WHEN SHALL WE EAT

Cake?

KELLEN BROOKS

When Shall We Eat Cake?

When Shall We Eat Cake?

Written by Kellen Brooks

Edited by Marcus Cylar & Karissa Johnson

ISBN: 978-0-9888030-3-9

When Shall We Eat Cake?

First Printing: 2019

ISBN: 978-0-9888030-3-9

Scripture quotations marked (NLT) are taken from the *Holy Bible*, New Living Translation, copyright ©1996. Used by permission of Tyndale House Publishers, Inc. Wheaton, Illinois 60189. All rights reserved.

Scripture quotations marked (NKJV) are taken from *The New King James Version Bible*. Nashville, TN: Thomas Nelson Publishers, 1975. All rights reserved.

Ordering Information: To purchase more paperback copies, e-books, and audio versions of the book, or for details on special discounts available on bulk purchases by corporations, associations, educators, and others, please contact the publisher at KellenBrooks.com

DEDICATION

On Friday, January 25, 2019 at 10:55pm, I lost a giant in my life. That was the day my grandfather passed away. My grandfather (Papa as I call him) has always been larger than life to me in more ways than one. Firstly, he was a tall man standing 6'2. But greater than his physical stature was his spiritual stature. He was a man of great faith, wisdom, humor and humility. My grandfather was easily one of the greatest men I have ever encountered. He taught me so many lessons throughout life by the words he said, the sermons he preached but most importantly, by the life that he lived.

Marriage was arguably one of Papa's favorite topics. He loved helping couples be at their best, especially reminding men "Love your wives as Christ loved the church." He and my grandmother enjoyed nearly 60 years of marital bliss and they are no doubt a huge inspiration behind my writing. I dedicate this book to their memory. Rest well, Isaac and Margaret King, Jr.

Kellen Brooks

When Shall We Eat Cake?

CONTENTS

Part III: When shall we eat cake?

ACKNOWLEDGMENTS

To all my friends and family who supported this vision and helped make this book a reality; whether you listened to the idea, gave feedback, or even helped me reach production; I appreciate you!

INTRODUCTION

A few years ago, I made a commitment to spend some more time communicating with my family. One way I planned to do this was by visiting my paternal grandparents. They only live about 20 minutes away from me, so it seemed like a pretty simple thing to do. I didn't realize how entertaining our time would be together!

During our visits, from the moment I walk in the door, my grandfather picks up with questions or discussion about the latest happenings, especially what's happening in our church world. We're all avid church goers, so that dominates much of our conversation. There is also a hot topic of discussion that usually alternates between my grandparents: marriage; particularly, *my* marriage. It's usually discussed in a roundabout way and introduced with the question,

"So Kellen, when are we going to eat cake?"

Whenever my grandma asks this, she just smiles and chuckles! I smile back, tickled at her questions and her roundabout way of asking me when I'm getting married. This question they ask is well-meaning and lighthearted. It isn't intrusive at all, nor do I get defensive when they ask. I just figure they're thinking, "Hey, you're getting up there, pal. When are you gonna lock something in with a young lady?" I'm sure they'd enjoy another great grandchild. My grandparents have been married for over 50 years. Their relationship is a miracle and I pray that one day, I am able to experience the longevity they are enjoying.

One day, something strange happened. While walking into the grocery store, this question just jumped into my head pretty randomly. I heard it clear as day, *When shall we eat cake?* The more I pondered this question, many questions began to flood my mind, particularly the questions single people usually get asked by their friends, family, associates, and maybe even strangers.

Like my grandparents' question to me, some of the questions and the people asking them are well-meaning and lighthearted. But there are other questions that just come off as intrusive and maybe even inappropriate. The more I thought about the "cake" question and other questions, I felt compelled to write. This book is the fruit of those questions that I hope to answer both practically and theologically where necessary.

The first section of this book looks at those questions and gives insight into their problematic nature. Some of the questions concerning why a person is still single are, at times, rooted in misconceptions of what makes a person prepared for marriage. It's my goal to explore some of these questions and give an answer.

The second section of this book looks at the types of questions that really matter–questions that single people should be asking another single person with whom they're pursuing something deeper. I call this series of questions the "C-Section" and I have categorized them into the following groups:

- Convictions: those ideas and practices that hold important moral value for yourself
- Circle: your relationship with your family, particularly your parents and friends
- Children: your views on children, having children, adopting children, treating others' children as your own children
- Cash: your views on money from saving and spending to giving
- Criminal past: your history of run ins with the criminal justice system
- Companions: your history of past relationships
- Confidence: how you understand fidelity and trust
- Calling: the collision of your passion and skills to meet the world's needs.
- Commitment to God: your faith and doctrinal beliefs

The third and final movement of this book unpacks the analogy for which the book is named, answering the question, *When shall we eat cake?* Cake is a metaphor for marriage. Each response plays upon that analogy and gives some insight into when it would be a good time to get married. From *finding a friend to enjoy cake with* to *not being afraid to break some eggs*, I believe you will find the insights clever and practical, easy to digest and understand.

Questions that can be asked to another single friend with whom you are dating or corresponding can be found on KellenBrooks.com. Most of these are light-hearted, basic information-seeking questions that break the ice.

Others are a little more in-depth and should probably only be asked in the event that the friendship is deepened or on the precipice of marriage.

As a single person who believes he is called to marriage, I am reading, musing, and applying these words myself. As it has been said, it's hard to trust a chef who doesn't eat his or her own cooking! I believe in the content provided and truly believe it will be an aid to anyone who reads it. Thanks for picking up this book. I pray you find it as a source of encouragement and wisdom in this great season of your life called singleness.

Part I: Questions People Ask Single People

When Shall We Eat Cake?

CHAPTER 1
ARE THERE NO GOOD GUYS OR GIRLS AROUND?

I'm sure you've heard this one before! There you are at the family reunion or the holiday dinner, talking with one of your elders. Perhaps you're chopping it up with one of your sassy aunts or old-school uncles. After talking about how grown you look now or even the few pounds you've put on (you already know family says whatever they want!), they inquire about your relationship status. When they find out you're not romantically involved with anyone, they hit you with that infamous question, *Are there no good guys (or girls) around?*

I believe there are a few inherent presuppositions in this question as it relates to the single person: (1) you are too picky, (2) you're not looking hard enough and (3) you're not positioning yourself well enough. Also, behind the question, is the obvious conclusion drawn by the person asking, that is, there *are* good people out there to date and eventually marry. Therefore, they conclude, because of some deficient behavior on your part, you're missing out on that good person.

You are too picky

The first assumption is, *You are too picky!* Can't you hear this ringing loudly underneath the question?

You have these standards, these dreams, this vision of the perfect person. Loosen up, they don't exist!

Pickiness refers to a highly critical and detailed standard we create to aid in our selection of a particular thing. Pickiness slims your options way down, or in an excessive case, eliminates all of them.

Of course, we can think back to earlier years when we painted in our minds this larger than life figure we would one day marry. You may have lessened up on that, which is ok. Over the years, I have significantly shifted my perspective on how I would define an amazing wife. My desires are a far cry from what I thought was a "dreamy" person in high school, even in college. But regardless to how your tastes, perspectives, likes and dislikes may change, those prerogatives belong solely to you. Who is to say that you are too picky? Have you taken the time to figure out what matters to you above what others try to define for you? I'll say this quite often throughout the book: the decision of whom you'll marry is your decision. One person may say "You're too picky!" but they don't have to live with your decision. They may know you well, but they don't know you as well as you know yourself.

Is being too picky a real thing? I believe so. But pickiness is a conclusion that a person has to arrive at themselves, absent of coaxing or manipulation of another. What's picky for one person or another will vary all the time whether in small or great degrees. However, we can measure our own pickiness by asking ourselves, "Am I holding someone to a standard that I myself do not uphold nor am striving to uphold?" If you can answer *Yes*, you are probably unjustifiably picky. I could be the one who says, "Lord, I want a supermodel" when the only fitness I do is "fit'ness whole pizza in my mouth" (I wish I could take credit for that line). Some of us will marry "out of our league" so to speak. But it shouldn't be our goal to hold high standards that we don't desire to meet. Conversely, if you have standards that you also are meeting or working towards, I venture to say that you are not too picky.

The reality is, there are tons of great people out there, but not every great person out there is your spouse. You can have a great time with a lot of people with fulfilling conversation, fun outings, and similar likes and interests. But those things alone aren't enough to help us make a lasting decision. The chemistry can be there, but as a good friend of mine put it, chemistry is not always equal to destiny. Pickiness is the line drawn to help you decipher between who may be good for you and who might be best for you.

You're not looking hard enough

A friend of mine was asked by an elderly gentleman, "Are you looking for a wife?" He replied, "No sir." The elderly gentleman then asked, "Are you married?" My friend grinned and responded, "No sir." Then the elderly man said rather matter-of-factly, "Well then, you're lookin'!"

During conversations like those, myself and other young men are likely to get hit with the Scripture, "He that findeth a wife findeth a *good thing…*" Proverbs 18:22.

Kellen, you gotta look if you gon' find!

What they're trying to say is "You're not trying hard enough." Frankly, I think some people are trying too hard. The other day I was in a restaurant and a reboot of an old-school dating show was on. I was amazed at how the show went about trying to contrive a love connection. One person, three dates, and a public digital scorecard used to grade the person's looks on a scale from one to 10 were all part of the sequence. I couldn't believe what I was watching. In my eyes, this was "trying too hard." It's ok to try and by try I mean meet a person, go out, and have a few conversations. There's nothing wrong with that. And through that experience something may spark, and then again, nothing may come of it. And that's perfectly fine. Casual dating isn't a *must* for finding someone, neither will I knock a person who goes on dates. Some prefer that route and take it a step further with the dating apps and dating profiles. That's not my cup of tea. It's hard enough getting to know people that are already in your social network (who you think you know already but really don't). It is especially an extreme risk getting to know someone with whom you have zero connection or history. Tread lightly with that! As my friend and I say facetiously, "Everybody on Christian Mingle ain't Christian and everybody on Tinder ain't tender!"

Regardless of the method you use, one shouldn't feel forced to take the casual dating route or be shamed into thinking they aren't trying hard enough. You can be minding your business, doing your work, living your life and experience an encounter without your coaxing, maneuvering and force. "Be still and know" can apply to a lot of things in life. In the quietness and stillness things can just flow our way. This doesn't mean that there will never be any effort on our part, but it does mean that we don't have to feel the pressure to work unnecessarily and make something happen. It may take longer, longer than usual, longer than culturally acceptable. However, I believe the less we try to make things happen in our own power and volition, the more space we give the Lord to work on our behalf.

When Abraham sent his servant to find a wife for his son Isaac, the servant made prayer a top priority. Genesis 24:12 says, "Then he said, 'O Lord God of my master Abraham, please give me success this day, and show kindness to my master Abraham.' "

He did not pursue a wife for Isaac without first pursuing God. He prayed that God would make his pursuit successful and he also prayed that God would show him the right person. Do you know that while he was praying, Isaac's bride to be showed up? I heard a quote which stated "A woman's heart should be so lost in God that a man needs to seek Him in order to find her." Make prayer a priority in your life. Pray for the spouse God has for you and pray that God won't let you make a mistake. Our first work is not showing up to a singles mixer, a social event, going on a tv show, or creating a dating profile. Our first work is seeking God through prayer.

When Isaac met his wife to be, he was not on a frantic search. Look at what the Bible says Isaac was doing,

Genesis 24:62-64
Now Isaac came from the way of Beer Lahai Roi, for he dwelt in the South. **63** And Isaac went out to meditate in the field in the evening; and he lifted his eyes and looked, and there, the camels *were* coming. **64** Then Rebekah lifted her eyes, and when she saw Isaac she dismounted from her camel;

Isaac was out in the field meditating in the evening time. Simply put, Isaac was spending some alone time fellowshiping with God. And while he was spending time with God, he looked up and saw his future wife and she saw him. It was a God-timed moment; a *kairos* moment, if you will. Now, I'm not promising a serendipitous meeting between you and your future spouse. But I am saying that when you make time for God, and set your affection on Him, He'll set your sights in the right direction.

You're not positioning yourself well enough

The last presupposition that could be lurking behind the question "Are there *no* good guys or girls around?" is that you're not positioning yourself well enough. This means that you're not showing up to the right places at the right times. You've heard it, "You've gotta get out there and mingle and let folk see you." There's some validity to that. Go out, have fun, attend events, go to a concert, etc. and you may be seen and possibly meet somebody. But just like the admonition to *try harder*, we can also fall into the web of exerting a lot of energy to be seen. Whether it's putting inordinate amounts of energy into our image, blocking off all of our weekends with social activities, "showing the right stuff" physically in order to gain some attention, and whatever acceptable or questionable behavior you can come up with; we can wear ourselves out by trying to be seen. I am an advocate for working on your image, your grooming, getting involved, and being sociable. For some people, those are extremely delightful activities. We should do these to the degree that we are comfortable, but also be aware that there are other things that catch people's eye beyond our appearance and our gregarious, outgoing nature.

Earlier, we talked about Abraham's servant who prayed before he found a spouse for Isaac. Within that prayer, he prayed to see some distinguishing actions.

Genesis 24:13-14
See, I am standing here beside this spring, and the young women of the town are coming out to draw water. **14** This is my

21

request. I will ask one of them, 'Please give me a drink from your container.' If she says, 'Yes, have a drink, and I will water your camels, too!'—let her be the one you have selected as Isaac's wife. This is how I will know that you have shown unfailing love to my master."

The servant's prayer was detailed so that God could give a sign validating his choice. He didn't pray for looks, but he did pray for someone that would not only serve but go the extra mile. Rebekah's offer was indeed an unusual one, "far beyond what human nature or the conventions of hospitality would dictate."[1] Her above average work ethic and hospitable nature is what caught the servant's eye and gave him the *green light* from God. Rebekah didn't go down to the well to find a husband. She went down to the well to get water, fulfilling her chores. No posturing or intentional positioning was done on her part. This incident teaches us that some unexpected things can happen in our favor when we just show up and take care of business. In the mundane and routine moments of our lives, God can develop something spectacular. God knows the right place and position for us. Just enjoy life, fulfill your purpose, do the routine but necessary things and you'll be surprised who and what God connects you to.

So, to answer the question of our good friends who ask us "Are there any good guys or girls around?" I answer with an emphatic *Yes!* There really are good guys and girls around and there is no pressure on us to find them. Sensitivity to the leading of the Lord and our own heart will let us know if we should rise up and go, 'be still and know,' or find some happy medium.

Signed, *A good guy*

---

[1] Keener, Craig S. and John H. Walton. *NRSV Cultural Backgrounds Study Bible*. Genesis 24:14. Grand Rapids, MI: Zondervan, 2019.

CHAPTER 2
ARE YOU HAVING SEX?

My grandfather, who was a pastor, would often give his testimony to the congregation relating to his marriage to my grandmother. He would tell us that he and his wife walked the aisle as virgins. That was burned in my mind as a child and has stuck with me through adulthood. Marrying as a virgin is a noble desire as is choosing a life of celibacy even after having had a sexual partner. During this season of singleness, I have learned a great deal about what it means to be sexually pure. Probably the most important lesson I've learned is that purity in body, although a good thing, is not the only thing. In fact, simply not having sex doesn't mean a person is sexually pure. Purity has to begin in the heart and then be followed by actions.

Sex is all around us. It's in the movies, commercials, music, and in conversations. It's everywhere. We are living in a hyper-sexualized culture. It is not uncommon to find people in church who are struggling with sexual sin, just like those outside of the Christian community. So when people see a single person in this sexualized world—even a Christian—they can't help but think that they must be engaging in some outlet for fulfilling sexual desire.

I have been asked on many occasions point blank: *Are you having sex? Have you had sex? Are you masturbating?* You may be thinking, *Wow, pretty intrusive! That's none of their business!* Yes, those can be really intrusive questions, especially from those with whom you do not have a personal relationship. This sort of questioning usually has less to do with the person being asked and is more of a reflection of the person asking the question.

One motivator for this question can, unfortunately, stem from a person's desire to see you fail. Perhaps they struggled in this area and they want you to experience the same struggle. Maybe it helps them not to feel inferior, soothing a personal insecurity thereby placing you both on a level playing field. This is a sad reality, as all have sinned and missed the mark (Romans 3:23). We are all in need of grace for sin, even sexual sin, whether we've had physical relations or we looked at people with a lustful eye (Matthew 5:28).

Projection can also fuel this type of question. This means that others ascribe to you certain ideas and feelings that they themselves may possess. People are very aware of their shortcomings and how they have navigated singleness unsuccessfully. They "tasted the fruit" and can't understand how you're not finding some outlet to quench sexual desires--as they may have during their single years. They may be thinking, *How are you able to do it?*

Lastly, at best, people ask these questions because they are just curious--dare I say it? Nosey. People want to know for their own reasons, whatever those may be. Then there are yet others who may just be seriously amazed at how a person can choose to live sexually pure in a sex-crazed world.

I remember in youth Bible studies years ago, one of the ministers tried to discourage us from kissing by saying that "A person could have a cut in their mouth, and if their blood gets in yours and they have AIDS, you may get it as well." I'm laughing as I type this, because while he was well meaning, it was just an absurd tactic to scare us out of kissing. He probably really believed his misinformed statement. Yes, his heart was in the right place for wanting us to live sexually pure lives on all fronts, but it just wasn't enough to keep us from going that route.

The threat of pregnancy or getting a disease is no longer enough motivation for people to abstain from sexual immorality. Even with those consequences looming, some feel like practicing abstinence is a losing battle. They figure since what has happened immorally can't be reversed and what *is* happening is too difficult to stop, why even try? I want to encourage you that there is never a bad time to start living sexually pure. Even with the challenges and negative influences that abound, you can live a chaste life. You can begin right where you are. It doesn't matter if you messed up last night or even moments ago. Start now and take one day at a time. The number of years you've been living pure and holy is not a trophy to be displayed or a "1 up" for your neighbor. The question is, can you stay saved all day? That's really all that matters. Take on *today*, and commit to living pure in your heart and your habits.

Strategies for living a sexually pure life

Holy Spirit

A person practicing abstinence, no matter if it's been 3 days or 3 years, doesn't do this in his/her strength alone. There are helpful strategies available for us to truly live a life of purity. I am reminded of a section from the Church Of God In Christ Statement of Faith, which my church recites:

> We believe in the sanctifying power of the Holy Spirit, by whose indwelling, the Christian is enabled to live a holy and separated life in this present world.[2]

In order to live the holy life, we need power beyond ourselves. We need the power and person of the Holy Spirit who will strengthen us to discipline ourselves, helping us say *no* to those inner desires and external

---

[2] http://www.cogic.org/about-company/statement-of-faith/

temptations for sexual sin. The Spirit will be our helper in those moments where will-power alone is not enough (Zechariah 4:6).

Holy Scripture

Scripture (the Bible, the Word of God) is one of the foremost weapons against sin in our lives. Meditating on the Word of God grants us success in everything we do, including living sexually pure (Joshua 1:8). Scripture, when embraced and meditated on, helps keep us from sin (Psalm 119:9, 11). The Word of God helps to shape our thoughts and understanding, which is the seed bed for either righteous or sinful living (Psalm 119:130). Since sexual purity begins in our hearts, when we are reframed in our thinking by meditating on the pure and holy Word of God, it will affect our actions for the good (Proverbs 23:7; Philippians 4:8; Matthew 5:28).

Boundaries

We need to set healthy boundaries in order to avoid sexual sin. Boundaries are dividing lines or limits that are set to restrict movement or behavior. There are usually a set of scenarios or behaviors that become a gateway for sexual sin to occur. Setting a boundary helps you to avoid the slippery slopes that could take you down the wrong path. Take personal note of those gateways and slippery slopes and commit to avoid the seemingly innocent scenarios that could cause you to stumble. Boundaries are not meant to simply restrict, but to give freedom.

A boundary allows you to move freely within a safe space, free of threat and worry. A dog gets a boundary such as a leash to keep him from going its own way. A child gets a boundary such as *don't go out in the street* to keep from getting hit by a car. Likewise, boundaries for your sexual purity will help give you the confidence and power to abstain.

Everyone's boundaries won't be the same (with exception of boundaries prescribed from Scripture), so it's important not to become legalistic about which boundaries you decided to take for yourself. A boundary may include a personal curfew, limits on when and where you can visit, monitoring what you watch, even cessation of communication when necessary. You know yourself better than anyone else, so be true to you and help keep yourself and others safe from damaging, sinful behavior.

Run!

We need a good "running game" to avoid sexual sin. Sometimes we need to physically remove ourselves from a situation or a scenario. At these moments, it's not about how *strong* you are to withstand the temptation. It's about honoring God, protecting our name, our testimony and the welfare of the other party.

The Bible records the story of a young man named Joseph in Genesis 39. Joseph was purchased as a slave and lived in the house of Potiphar. Joseph found favor with his master Potiphar, thus becoming the manager of Potiphar's entire household. Nothing was withheld from Joseph's oversight, except for Potiphar's wife. One day, Potiphar's wife began to press Joseph to sleep with her. He turned down her advances and expressed, "How then can I do this great wickedness, and sin against God?" (Genesis 39:9b). Day after day she propositioned him, but Joseph would not yield. One day, while no one else was home, she grabbed Joseph by his clothing and demanded he lie with her. But he left his clothing and ***ran outside***. Words were no longer enough. Joseph had to lace up his cross trainers and run! Paul gave very similar advice to a young pastor named Timothy,

> 2 Timothy 2:22
> Run from anything that stimulates youthful lusts. Instead, pursue righteous living, faithfulness, love, and peace. Enjoy the companionship of those who call on the Lord with pure hearts.

Some things you can't reason with; you have to run from it. Running doesn't make you a coward. Running makes you wise.

These tools are available to anyone who wants them. As believers, we should actually believe what the Bible says and know that we have the power to live above sin in our lives. There are people abstaining from fornication and living successful Christian lives by the grace of God.

Before we ask such personal questions related to a person's sexual behavior, we should ask ourselves:

- Is it necessary for me to know this information? If no, don't ask. If yes, why?
- How will this information help or hinder my relationship with this person?
- Will I be tempted to tell someone this personal information? If yes, don't ask.
- Is this a person I'm dating, considering for marriage, or have a personal relationship with? If no, don't ask.

If you are the recipient of such a question, you can always choose not to answer. Not answering the question does not mean you're guilty. You have a right to keep certain things private and release information only when necessary or bearing on the relationship you are currently in. A good friend once told me, "Always tell the truth but don't always be tellin' it!" His sentiments were that we should be honest with people but we should avoid oversharing and offering too much information.

CHAPTER 3
YOU'RE GOOD LOOKING! WHY HAVEN'T YOU FOUND SOMEONE YET?

Single, pastor, musician, *and* a working man. Those are some very loose terms which describe me but, quite frankly, they don't tell you a whole lot about who I am. I must admit, it is a little flattering when people add another descriptor to the list: handsome. Now, I didn't say this about myself. "They" said it about me. But it's what follows after that statement that becomes troubling:

"You're handsome! Why aren't you married?"
The implication is that good looks, or perceived good looks, are a fundamental criterion for getting married. Some feel that people who are judged as *good looking* somehow have a greater advantage or entitlement to finding a spouse. I'd be putting on a facade if I didn't admit to seeing someone attractive and thinking "Hmm, they're not involved?" But I realize that this attitude is very unfortunate and problematic.

Beauty is relative.

I saw a fake news article which reported that a woman was suing her parents for 2 million dollars because she blames them for her ugliness. I must tell you, that's probably one of the most absurd (and funny) things I've ever read. Although fake, it points to a sad reality. There are people who are discouraged because of their perceived lack of beauty.

People hold varying standards and degrees for what they consider to be attractive. As the old adage goes, "Beauty is in the eye of the beholder" which means that "beauty cannot be judged objectively, for what one person finds beautiful or admirable may not appeal to another."[3] Each person has their own perception of what constitutes aesthetic beauty. It is not helpful to place these perceptions and standards on others. However, in many ways, both subtle and overt, people are encouraged to conform to a specific standard of beauty. Straight hair or crinkly hair. Dark skin or lighter skin. Chiseled physique or less defined physiqued. Exaggerated body parts or average. Long hair, short hair, no hair. We all have differing ideas of what is beautiful and yet there is a unique and innate beauty to be found in everyone as image bearers of God.[4] How do aesthetics in any way show that a person is ready to be married or even should be married? Beauty does matter, but it is a minor factor in the grand scheme.

Beauty is fading.

Proverbs 31:30 (NKJV)

Charm is deceitful and beauty is passing, but a woman who fears the Lord, she shall be praised.

We all know that beauty changes shape and definition. We may be *supermodel status* in our 20s but a radically different image in our 60s. Things change. People change. We get blemishes, wrinkles, and gravity gets the best of us. Hair turns gray and falls out. Strength and desire wane. Beauty, as we know it, is constantly fading. Therefore, leaning towards marriage because of beauty is not wise and not strong enough to sustain the rigors of marriage.

Going beneath the surface

---

[3] Google search: define "beauty is in the eye of the beholder."
[4] Genesis 1:26, Ephesians 2:10

I believe most people have a desire to be their best and look their best. This is healthy and I encourage this. How we see ourselves and present ourselves will affect how others see and interact with us. But when we are solely focused on physical beauty we will place an unhealthy confidence in how we look. Our identity is more than skin deep. You are not your hair, your clothes, your jewelry or your body type. Those things will come and go. Consider more than just your physical image and ask yourself, "How can I cultivate my inner beauty?" 1 Peter 3:3-5 speaks to wives specifically, but its applications can apply to any member of the body of Christ.

> Don't be concerned about the outward beauty of fancy hairstyles, expensive jewelry, or beautiful clothes. **4** You should clothe yourselves instead with the beauty that comes from within, the unfading beauty of a gentle and quiet spirit, which is so precious to God. **5** This is how the holy women of old made themselves beautiful…(NLT)

The main point is that inner beauty holds greater and lasting weight compared to outward beauty. Even God emphasized this point when preparing to choose a new king for Israel. He sent the prophet Samuel on a mission to the house of a man named Jesse, to anoint another king in place of the current king, Saul. Jesse brought out his oldest son Eliab. After one look, Samuel said to himself, "This has got to be the new king!" Jesse had many sons and brought them one by one in front of Samuel. Samuel made assumptions about who the king was because of the external build and presence. But God told Samuel in no uncertain terms,

> "Look not on his countenance, or on the height of his stature; because I have refused him: for the Lord seeth not as man

seeth; for man looketh on the outward appearance, but the
Lord looketh on the heart." 1 Samuel 16:7

In the Garden of Eden, God placed two trees, the Tree of Life
and the Tree of the Knowledge of God and Evil.[5] God gave
instructions not to eat from the Tree of the Knowledge of Good and
Evil, because in the day they ate of it, they would certainly die. One day,
the serpent engaged in conversation with Eve, enticing her to eat from
the tree that God had forbidden. Eve was convinced and decided to eat
it. Listen to how the writer describes this enticing moment in Genesis
3:6-7:

> The woman was deceived. She saw that the tree was **beautiful**
> and its fruit looked delicious, and she wanted the wisdom it
> would give her. So she took some of the fruit and ate it. Then
> she gave some to her husband, who was with her, and he ate it,
> too. **7** At that moment their eyes were opened, and they
> suddenly felt shame at their nakedness. So they sewed fig leaves
> together to cover themselves.

Eve was enamored with the physical, outward beauty of the tree
and its fruit, but it was a deadly meal. She couldn't tell by the outside
that what she would partake of would be detrimental to her both
spiritually and naturally. Although this was a different context, the
principle stands as it relates to beauty. Just because something is
pleasing to the eye, doesn't mean it possesses sustaining fruit. As I have
heard it growing up, *Everything that looks good to you, ain't good for you!*
Beauty has to go beyond what we see; it cannot be the measure for
marital preparedness. Ultimately, God looks at the heart and knows the
inner things that can be developed and cultivated in us before we add
another person to the equation.

---

[5] Genesis 2:9

CHAPTER 4
DON'T YOU WANT TO MARRY AND HAVE CHILDREN BEFORE YOU'RE TOO OLD?

Have you ever had a timeline in your mind for when you would accomplish certain things in your life? Graduate by *this* age, have a certain type of job by *that* age, have your bank account at a particular number by *this* age, and of course be married by *that* age. Maybe *this* age and *that* age has already come. You may have passed those ages and you're well into your late twenties, thirties or forties, patiently waiting, maybe even wondering if this will happen for you. While it is quite possible that you may ultimately have the "gift of singleness," many others will get married and some of us will take a little longer than others to finally walk down the aisle.

Maybe you don't have a particular target age for marriage, which would be a good thing in my opinion. Not pressuring yourself to meet an age deadline for marriage–an event that is not entirely dependent on you–will certainly help you to manage your expectations and minimize disappointment. Whether you have a set age or not, there are people, unbeknownst to you, that have picked out an age *they* think you should be married by.

One day I was attending a Christmas event for pastors and their spouses. Each leader was invited to give a personal introduction then introduce their spouse. It was my turn and I got up to make my introduction. Of course, being single, I had no spouse to introduce and I made a light-hearted humorous reference to my lack of spousal support. The audience got a chuckle out of it and one person shouted out "Take your time." Immediately, an older woman attending responded, "Don't you take your time. You need a wife!" In essence she was telling me to hurry up and get on it, because I'm getting older and time is fleeting. I had to laugh again at that advice!

Take your time. Hurry up!

Using age as a strong motivator for when a person should get married could present a major issue that some couples have had to grapple with: rushing in. If marriage is rushed beyond a person's desire, it is usually fueled by people pleasing. *They* said you should do it. *They* said you're getting old. *They* are waiting for grandchildren. In his sermon series and book *Fifty Shades of They*, Pastor Ed Young describes the importance of having the right *they* in your life; that is, the right group of people who will positively influence your life. The wrong *they* will criticize you, pressure you, and potentially harm you by their words and presence. The right *they* will be a source of strength and encouragement for you. Pastor Young cleverly stated, "The wrong *they* will have you in a fray!"[6]

Which *they* are you listening to in your life concerning your future? *They* may have a lot of opinions. *They* may have a lot of suggestions. *They* may even be well meaning, but *they* won't be around when you and *bae* become one! So take *they* with a grain of salt when you feel the pressure mounting. Now, I don't want you to think that I'm advocating for you to minimize the suggestions and input of people in your life who care about your well being and want to see you happily married. But I am encouraging you to consider your desires and your

---

[6] Young. Ed. *Fifty Shades of They: Choose - Part 1*. Sermon published, January 11, 2015. <https://youtu.be/VirGaFTDyiM>.

own waiting process above someone's personal thoughts about your age and marriage.

A woman shared her wedding story with me a few years ago that really caught my attention. For years, she had been patiently waiting on God to send her a spouse. She was a lovely lady, active in her church, and she loved the Lord, but it seemed like *Mr. Right* just wouldn't come. On top of her waiting, she was celibate and remained a virgin. Practicing abstinence is a challenge by itself, but she was practicing well into her 40s! That's an admirable feat to say the least. It was not until she was in her forties that God would send her a spouse. She had her first child at age 46! Yes, she waited for a long time, but did not count out the possibility of getting married and having children, even at her age. Yes, she will be older raising her child. She'll be in her 60s when the child is in high school, perhaps in her 70s when that child gets married and quite possibly in her 80s when she has her first grandchild. And what's wrong with that? Not one thing. Yes, it would be great to have your prime years to run after your children, grandchildren and such, but we don't know what God has in store for us who wait on Him.

On another occasion, I met a lady who was over 100 years old. What she told me put a smile on my face and laughter in my heart. She said, "I'm going to invite you to my wedding when I get engaged!" She has made her transition to her heavenly home, but she didn't see her age as a factor. If anyone thought she was too old, it certainly wasn't herself! I don't plan to be 100 when I wed, but age shouldn't pressure us to make a permanent decision we're not ready for nor desiring at the moment.

The marrying age has increased over many years. In the 20th century, the median age for marriage was at its lowest in 1956. The median age for men and women marrying for the first time was 22.5 and 20.1 respectively.[7] During this time, there were many people

---

[7] https://www.census.gov/population/socdemo/hh-fam/tabMS-2.pdf

marrying during their teenage years and early twenties. Even into the early 21st century, the median age for men and women reached 27.1 and 25.3 respectively. The trend we've seen is that most people, historically speaking, get married before they reach their thirties. With these numbers in mind, it's no wonder that people use age as a barometer for marital preparedness, citing those in their 30s as getting "old."

Getting married older than usual will disappoint those who desire to live vicariously through you. In my case, I know that the treasured people in my life who mention my age and their timeclock for me to be married only want the best for me. They desire to see me with energy and vitality in raising children and want me to be *safe*, that is, free from the sexual temptations that await a single man. Then there are others who may just want me to fit their mold. Once, it was brought to my attention that a disgruntled member felt I shouldn't be a pastor because I'm not married and I have no children. "How can he rule his house well with no children?" was their point of contention. People will come up with all sorts reasons as to why you need to go ahead and tie the knot. Whatever position you find yourself in when people bring up your age, know that at the end of the day, God's timing is not ours. It is your life and your decision, which is influenced by God's timing. Remember, you have to sleep in the bed you make. So let the years roll on and don't let age be an unnecessary pressure for moving into marriage.

PART II: THE C SECTION CATEGORIES OF QUESTIONS SINGLE PEOPLE SHOULD ASK WHILE DATING

When Shall We Eat Cake?

CHAPTER 5
CONVICTIONS

Some years ago I was at my mechanic's shop getting some work done to my tan Mercury Sable. Being at the shop was much like being at the neighborhood barbershop. There were always questions and conversations to be had. They knew I was a young preacher and an avid church goer, so the conversation naturally covered church issues from time to time. This time, the conversation centered on "church clothes." One mechanic (we'll call him Joe) was not a believer but had strong ideas about appropriate church wardrobe. He told me with disdain about a pastor's wardrobe at a church he attended. Joe grumbled, "This pastor was in the pulpit preaching with a baseball cap on! You ain't supposed to be no pastor with a hat on in church!"

For Joe, he had a strong conviction about how a pastor should look and dress in church. He was pretty adamant about the reverend not wearing a hat indoors and visibly showed his disdain for the practice. I found the conversation rather comical, but it really mattered to Joe.

What principles in life are you adamant about upholding? Like Joe, what *no no's* get you riled up and passionate when others engage them? One word can describe these feelings: convictions.

A conviction is a fixed or firmly held belief. Convictions frame how you think and conduct yourself. They also play a part in framing your expectations of how others live and conduct themselves. Whether we have named them or not, we all have convictions and fixed ideas that influence how we live. Your political ideas, faith, friendships, work ethic, relationships, and health are just a few things that are shaped by your convictions. We will find ourselves most closely connected to those individuals who share the same foundational convictions.

The convictions of people of faith grow out of their relationship with God, God's Word, and the faith traditions they are formed in (i.e. denominations, churches, groups, etc.). Things such as how we treat each other, how we treat people of other ethnicities, how we plan to raise our children, our ideas concerning use of alcohol/drugs, our view the planet and our responsibility to it, how we plan to spend our money, and other issues are closely related to how we understand our faith and how we live it out.

When foundational convictions cannot be agreed upon, there is bound to be turbulence in the relationship and marriage. People with similar convictions will make the best spouses for each other. Be sure to ask the questions concerning your convictions to see if these are foundational or secondary things. Consider these additional topics not mentioned above:

- What are your thoughts on pornography?
- How far is too far or what is acceptable before marriage?
- Will you kiss before your married?
- How do you feel about LBGT+ lifestyles? Ok or not ok?
- Have you had a previous relationship with someone of the same sex?
- Pro life or pro choice?
- Is church attendance important or not so much?
- Vacations: Are they a necessity or luxury?
- Time alone vs. time together: Is there ever a time we need to be alone?
- Dancing. Is it ever appropriate?
- How do you interpret husbands love your wives or wives obey your husbands?

- Modest dress: What boundaries do you have for what is/isn't appropriate?
- Tattoos: To ink or not to ink?
- Language: How do you feel about profanity usage verbally and through text acronyms?
- Physical health: Is exercise important? Are plastic surgery, tummy tucks, implants, etc. ok?

You may even have your own questions to add to this list. These are just some questions to get you started thinking about your own personal convictions and how they may or many not compliment the person you're interested in. Your convictions may seem silly to some, but if they matter to you, they matter. Let no one talk you out of the things that matter most to you. Bending on a tightly held conviction in order to accomodate someone else may put you in a compromising spot if not a very uncomfortable one. Yes, we will grow in our beliefs and understanding over time on some issues, but it is best to go into any serious relationship on very similar pages concerning convictions.

CHAPTER 6
CIRCLE

Friends

Tell me about your two or three closest friends.

The way people act, think, and reason is most often a composite of the individuals they share intimate space with. In other words, you can learn a lot about a person from the types of friends they have. What do they talk about? What interests them? What activities do they do together? How do they deal with people? While looking at a person's friends doesn't give you a completely accurate assessment of that person's character, it definitely gives a glimpse into what that person tolerates, values, and commits to. People don't tend to make *close* friends with those who starkly contrast their deep seated convictions and practices, therefore, it's safe to assume that birds of a feather *still* flock together.

If a person says they have no close friends it's good to inquire why. Close friends can be hard to come by and you do well to have a couple of people you can invest deeply with. However, if a person has *no* close friends, that may reveal a deeper personal issue, character flaws, or insecurity.

Family

How's your relationship with your parents? Siblings? Which parent are you closer to and why? How were you raised? Who was the disciplinarian?

Marrying a person undoubtedly connects you to their family. Your future spouse's siblings become your siblings, his parents become your parents. Her crazy uncle is now "our crazy uncle." People will bring into relationships, to a very large degree, the values and examples that were set before them by their familial relationships. Guys will likely repeat what they learned from their father or male figures in their lives concerning gender roles and treating women. Likewise, young women will bring to the table their understanding of how women and men should function. Those understandings may include expectations that may not be widely held but were prevalent in her home (i.e. who does the cooking, takes out the trash, pays the bills, etc.). Learning about each other's family and relationships with those immediate and close family members will give you insight into what you can expect, should the friendship blossom into something more. I come from a big family (I am one of 7 children), but yet home is personal space for me. I have no problem walking in, saying "hello" and sitting to myself the rest of the day. Others may have a totally different experience. It's good to talk about those sorts of dynamics to minimize the surprises and manage expectations in a future marriage.

There are many questions one could ask regarding a person's circle of family and friends. In addition to what's mentioned above, it's important to ask if their parents were divorced. In his book, *Before We Say I Do,* Dr. Marvin McMickle influences potential mates to "consider whether an earlier experience of divorce has, in any way, influenced your views about marriage."[8] Just as others values and expectations are "caught" through family dynamics, it could be that the experience of a

---

[8] McMickle, Marvin. *Before We Say I Do: 7 Steps to a Healthy Marriage.* Valley Forge, PA.: Judson Press, 2003. page 97.

divorce can have both negative and positive effects on a person's understanding of marriage.

My parents divorced when I was around 4 years old. The majority of my life was lived around my mother and my grandparents. What I learned about family and marriage was, to a great degree, shaped by what I saw in my maternal grandparents. Because of their example, I determined at a very young age that I would go into marriage as a virgin and stay married no matter what obstacles would arise. Outside of living with my grandparents, I also saw first hand what it's like growing up in a single parent home, having to mature earlier than needed and bear more responsibility because there was no father in the home. Those experiences have helped mold me and produced certain useful qualities. Nevertheless, I don't want my children to have to ever go through those experiences. It's important to share those same convictions concerning marriage and divorce with whom you'll marry. Be alarmed if a person sees divorce as a viable option for solving disagreements and disputes that will arise in a marriage. A healthy discussion on this topic will prove invaluable.

There will be enough surprises as it is after saying "I do." Talking about these fundamental elements concerning a person's circle helps to build a good foundation and avoid potential hiccups in the future.

CHAPTER 7
CHILDREN

Behold, children are an heritage of the Lord: and the fruit of
the womb is his reward.
Psalm 127:3

To me there is no picture so beautiful as smiling, bright-eyed, happy
children; no music so sweet as their clear and ringing laughter.
P. T. Barnum

In a culture that draws further away from having children and
looks with skepticism at those who, in contemporary times, produce big
families, the Bible views children as a blessing from God. The psalmist
calls children a "heritage" which means an inheritance. Children are
gifts from God that belong to Him and he has invited parents on the
incredible journey of stewarding those precious gifts by raising them,
providing for them, and training them in the ways of the Lord. God
gave a mandate to the first couple to be fruitful and multiply, to fill the
earth. Even with such a mandate, couples have freedom in how this is
played out in their marriage.

There are a myriad of questions to consider concerning
children. Will you have children right away or wait a while after getting
married? Where do each of you stand on the use of contraceptives?
Will you have a small family, medium sized, or large family with many
children? Will you explore adoption if infertility or health becomes an
impediment to having children? Is having any children at all a goal for

you? Are you open to marrying someone with children and acting as a "bonus" parent?

Serious discussion should be given to this matter as not all people will see eye to eye on the topic of children and what being "fruitful and multiplying" looks like. Always be flexible as it relates the discussion of children. The miracle of child bearing comes from God and God has given many "surprises" to married couples who thought they planned and had everything figured out. Plan and discuss, but also know that God can circumvent even the most planned and executed agendas when pregnancies early in the marriage.

CHAPTER 8
CASH

A feast is made for laughter, wine makes life merry, and money is the answer for everything.
Ecclesiastes 10:19

"Romance without finance is a nuisance...It aint' no joke to be broke!"
From the song, ***"Romance Without Finance"***

An older gentleman with 40 years of marriage under his belt was sure to let me know that if you're going to do the married life successfully, you're going to need some money. Money is definitely an important topic of discussion prior to marriage. Now, I wouldn't suggest bringing up money until things are very serious relationally. Some questions, which are vital, I believe are best reserved for the premarital counseling stage; questions such as credit scores and annual income. However, there are other questions I believe to be safe and appropriate prior to that stage, such as:

- Do you have a job? Any career aspirations?
- How would you best describe your money practices? Spender, saver, giver?
- Do you use a budget?
- Do you believe in tithing, giving 10% of your income to church?
- What kind of debt do you have if any?

Men and women may have different views in terms of how provisions for the home will be made. Neglecting to discuss this issue ahead of time could result in strong disagreements and failed expectations. Feel free to ask these types of questions:

- Do you see the man as the primary breadwinner?
- Should household expenses be shared?
- How do you view the ownership of a couple's money?

In relation to the last question, some will see ownership of money in different ways. One view is that all the money is "our" money, no matter how much one makes. Another view is that money earned individually may be seen as the sole ownership of the person who worked for it (i.e. You have your money and I have mine). Or some may even say "What's mine is mine and what's yours is mine." There may even be a mix of these positions. Whichever way you view it, that's an important discussion to have and get clarity on. Don't shy away from the money talks!

CHAPTER 9
CRIMINAL PAST

Many stories abound of a person that escaped the law earlier in life only for the past to catch up with them. A few years ago, a story emerged about a lady who escape from a Michigan jail. She moved to the West Coast, changed her name and started a whole new life. After marrying, bearing children, and evading the law for 37 years, her past finally caught up with her. A few leads and picture led police right to her home. Needless to say, it was a shock to her family.

Unlike the corporate world, you can't issue background checks on those you are getting to know better or dating. It will then be incumbent upon each of you to be transparent about you criminal past to avoid any potentially devastating information rising to the surface. With public documents lingering online, a quick google search may reveal more information than you're willing to share! It's best to be up front when the time presents itself.

What's in your criminal past that could potentially affect your present? Asking questions on this topic is not to satisfy a person's indulgence for private information or to cause shame and embarrassment. God forgives and cleans our slate, so questions about criminal past shouldn't be seen as fault finding and rehashing previous issues that have been dealt with. Rather, these sorts of questions help a person to weigh the impact of past decisions on the couple's future together. The types of crimes committed could reveal aspects of the person's character that could go unnoticed. Yes, people can change, but there are others who have latent issues or struggles that are connected to their past criminal actions. Violent crimes, sexual offenses, drug and alcohol related offences, traffic offences, financial crimes, etc. could offer a glimpse into a person's character. These are not *just-getting-to-know-you* questions, but these questions are reserved for friendship that is more serious, nearing or at the point of engagement.

No area concerning your criminal past should be off limits. If there is hesitation from the person being asked these questions or if there seems to be more to the story that what is shared, take concern. If necessary, see it as a big red flag. Issues of transparency and trust early on will only intensify after the marriage. So build confidence by sharing about criminal past, no matter how embarrassing it may feel or has been. You'll be glad you asked and answered those difficult questions.

CHAPTER 10
COMPANIONS

The country song just popped into my head, *All My Ex's Live in Texas.*

> *All my ex's live in Texas.*
> *And Texas is the place I'd dearly love to be.*
> *But all my ex's live in Texas.*
> *And that's why I hang my hat in Tennessee.*[9]

If you don't have an ex or any past romantic interest, consider yourself fortunate. You are part of a minority within a large pool of single people. Why should you consider yourself fortunate? You have avoided unnecessary conflict, confusion, heartbreak, misunderstanding, and very plainly, wasted time. However, having no romantic history is likely not the experience of most single people. Past relationships can definitely have bearings on how a person operates within a new relational space, which is why the subject of past companions is an important one to cover.

The single most important question concerning past companions is, "Have you ever been married?" Divorce is a big deal and a previous marriage is the most obvious past relationship that should be discussed. Those who have experienced divorce know that the severance of a marital union is never a clean cut. It always leaves

---

[9] Sanger D. Shafer and Lyndia J. Shafer (1987). *All My Ex's Live in Texas*. Recorded by George Strait on the album *Ocean Front Property*.

jagged edges on the hearts of those involved, no matter how smooth the divorce may have seemed. Marrying a divorcee may or may not be a deal breaker for the person you are pursuing. That's one area you don't want to keep a secret or wait until you are asked about. Get ahead of the question and bring it up if you are the person who has experienced a divorce.

Not to insult your intelligence, but let's define divorce. Divorce is the legal dissolving of a marriage. It's important for us to note this definition because being separated from your spouse is not equal to being divorced from your spouse. Many have found themselves involved with someone who was still married yet separated. That would be adultery and should be avoided at all costs. Nothing good comes from being in a romantic relationship with a married person, no matter what stage the marriage is in.

Should you find out that the person with whom you are corresponding is married, cease and desist! It could be that God will restore that person's marriage, so don't act out of season. If for no other reason, respecting the marriage covenant and God's standard is reason enough not to entertain any relationship with a married person even when he or she is separated.

As a close second to asking about divorce, I would encourage you to ask if a person has ever been engaged to be married or involved in any serious relationships. Follow up those questions with *Why did those relationships fail?* and *What was learned from those experiences?*

Asking questions about a person's relational past can give you some insight into the character and practice of that person. We are the common denominator in our previous romances and dating relationships; so if there are patterns repeated from those relationships, they can possibly be revealed with candid conversation. Asking about past companions can also show you how that person has dealt with conflict and disappointment. How a person has handled these sort of situations in the past can be a reliable indicator of how they'll handle similar scenarios in the future.

The last question regarding companions deals with sexual history. The question is very simple: *Have you had sex?* It really doesn't get any more direct than that. As things progress and become more serious in a relationship, it's important to ask the sexual history questions. Is a person's sexual history something that you could handle and look past or will it create apprehension? No person has to be tethered to their past if they have changed their ways and repented of past misconduct. Neither should we hold people's past over their heads. But people should have the opportunity to both share and know what they are getting into. You should not feel guilty for opting out of the dating phase because of a person's sexual past. Don't ignore your apprehensions or feel manipulated to stick with it. Opting out does not make you wrong, judgemental or closed-minded. Rather, it allows you to hold true to your convictions and operate honestly with yourself and the person you're getting to know.

If a person's sexual history is an issue for you now, it will likely be an issue for you later. On the other hand, honesty about sexual history may have the opposite effect. A person may gain deeper trust with you and be at ease with your past. Either conclusion is fine and acceptable. Just be sure that you're comfortable with the decision to keep moving forward or bow out.

Because this topic of sexual history is so sensitive, things will likely be uncomfortable and awkward during the conversation, *especially* if one person's past is spotted with sexual experiences and the other person's is not. This conversation should not be avoided because of its nature, but should be discussed in the most non-judgemental and gentle way as possible.

When having the conversation about past relationships, be sensitive about when to ask. I believe asking about a person's marital history should happen rather quickly, while questions about ex's in general should probably wait. Some rapport should be built before the questions about relationships probe too deeply (other than asking if the person has been married). When having these conversations, ask yourself:

- How does he talk about his past relationship?
- Is there indignation, displeasure or resolve in his voice as he discusses a failed relationship?
- Does she seem to still be working through the loss of an ex or appear to have overcome it?

Being honest in your assessment of these conversations will help you determine if you really want to continue getting to know this person or pump the brakes. This sort of conversation is able to build trust, especially if the person recounting this history balances the story.[10] A balanced story contains an honest assessment of a person's own mistakes and lessons they've learned, not just the shortcomings of the ex in question.

It is possible to discuss the core of those experiences without sharing excessive details or airing the business of the other individuals who were involved. Try to keep from exposing others when talking about your own past relationships with a new person. The purpose of having conversations about previous companions is not to taint the image of your ex or remain in the past, but to gain insights to help you navigate the road ahead.[11] These conversations are the building blocks for a potentially promising future. Kudos to those who dare to take the bold step and have the hard conversations about the past. Things will fare better because of it.

---

[10] Adams, Rebecca. "Here's Why You Should Talk To Your Partner About Your Ex (Seriously)." HuffPost, 1 July 2014,
https://www.huffpost.com/entry/talking-about-your-ex_n_5533210.
[11] ibid.

CHAPTER 11
CONFIDENCE

As children, we came into the world with an uncanny ability to trust. We held on to every word we were told. We took seriously even the most bizarre claims. Why? Because we were wired to believe and trust recklessly. But over time, the ability to freely trust is hampered. Broken promises, betrayed confidence, and failed expectations build up a callous around our hearts, making it more difficult to trust others. The heart that cannot trust is a heart that will grow cold and closed.

For any friendship to thrive, it must have as its foundation a mutual trust and confidence shared by both parties. There are enough people and situations in our lives that lure us toward suspicion, skepticism, and insecurity. The last place we want to feel those negative emotions is with a person we are building friendship with. Because of the great role trust plays in relationships, it's important to get an understanding of how each other views trust and the degree to which you can place confidence in each other. There are a few questions that I place under this umbrella of confidence in an effort to show the different ways in which we measure trust, holding information, and publicizing things.

Some questions I will address include:

- How do you handle private information?
- How free are you with your personal life on social media?
- What does fidelity look like to you in light of opposite sex friendships?

How do you handle secrets, private information, or other people's business?

People will usually show you better than they can tell you as it relates to how they hold information. Take this scenario for instance. You may casually share some information with someone and did not expressly ask to keep it confidential. But the other person may be more open in their communication, whose inner circle is much wider than yours. So, in sharing something that you may have seen as an exclusive story, it then becomes the news that Momma, Daddy, brother, sister, cousin, and aunt are all aware of. He or she may not have seen it as a betrayal of trust, and honestly that may be too harsh of a description for the nature of the information shared. You just figured it would be something that would stay between the two of you. The other person could see it as a casual sharing of what's going on in their relational world that's fair game for sharing with others. Apparently, there are two different views on how confidence in one another looks. This could be potentially be a major problem if not addressed and discussed.

How does your friend treat other people's business? It has been said that if a person will tell you the intimate details of someone else's life, then they'll tell your business to someone else as well. I have a hard time believing a lot of people would own up to revealing their tendency to share information that should be kept private, so you must simply watch for the type of conversation they have with you. If too many intimate details are shared with you about others, be on guard.

How free are you with your personal life on social media?

About a decade ago, I was a little more free with what I posted and said on social media. I described a playful incident that took place in my home and referred to a visiting family member without saying her name. Well, someone read the post, and then reported back to my family member who wasn't on Facebook. I noticed this family member began to act a little out of character and wasn't her usual cordial self. Things seemed sort of weird, so I said something to break the ice. It was then that I discovered that she was disappointed in what I shared. It was lighthearted and I didn't see it the way she saw it. After having to explain myself, clear things up and apologize, I made a commitment to keep what I posted on social media general and not so intimate. That incident and others have definitely changed me into an ultra private person, perhaps sometimes to the extreme. Nonetheless, privacy is my new normal. What's done at home is done in confidence, with some reasonable exceptions. Now, there are others who post about everything–pictures, location, scenarios and the list goes on and on. They go "live" anywhere, the bedroom, the boardroom, and dare I say it...the bathroom. No exaggeration here. A private person and a social person will have different views on confidentiality when it comes to social presence. What may be ok for one could be a nightmare for the other!

What does fidelity look like to you in light of opposite sex friendships?

Exclusivity and monogamy are unspoken standards in a committed relationship and marital relationship. Those standards can be compromised with inappropriate opposite-sex friendships. To be fair, there are some opposite-sex friendships that are unavoidable and necessary to a person's life such as friendships with coworkers, church members, or people you are working on projects with. Secure people will realize that their significant other or spouse will have people of the opposite sex in their social circle. But there are other opposite-sex friendships that can prove harmful even without there being a physical, sexual transgression. These types of friendships are questionable and could make the person you're getting to know very uneasy.

I am convinced that how a person navigates opposite-sex friendships while in committed relationships or even in the middle of working towards one reveals much about their character and the level at which they can be trusted. One's behavior with opposite-sex friendships before marriage is not bound to change simply because vows have been exchanged. These habits are not broken overnight so it's best to work on that now. If one doesn't manage those interactions before "I do," issues are bound to show up and cause strife. Those who take seriously the marriage vows will exercise restraint and show a change in friendships because of their commitment to the vows and desire for fidelity.

A loss of confidence in a person doesn't need something as serious as cheating in a relationship or adultery in a marriage to take place. Confidence can be lost based on how people view their roles in the development of opposite-sex friendships. The scope of this book doesn't tackle that issue in depth but to put it succinctly, some people thrive off of flirtatious interactions and have a hard time turning the behavior off. People could be committed but yet find thrill in the potential of an extra connection. A betrayal of trust can happen simply because a man or woman gives a person outside of the relationship hope that something could develop.[12] A person who is serious about their commitment will actively shut down advancements that could harm what they're trying to build with someone else.

When a person shows this side of their character, believe them. They may not see their behavior as an issue. For them, they are operating within the bounds of trust. But for you, dissuading potential friendships that can divert your attention away from the core friendship is part of building trust. Once again, questions surrounding where you

---

[12] Rev. Dr. Howard John Wesley proposed this idea in a Q&A Bible Study session called CAYA, at Alfred Street Baptist Church in Spring/Summer 2018.

stand on these matters will reveal if these actions are something you can cope with or if they are, unequivocally, dealbreakers.

When Shall We Eat Cake?

Chapter 12
Calling

What's your calling in life?

I see calling as the collision of your passion, skills, and the world's needs. This goes deeper than just a career or the current job a person works, although a calling can be evident in those things. Calling is that special work in which you are so motivated to do that you'll do it for free and even lose sleep in the process. Whether we are aware of it or not, we all have a calling.

I don't think a person has to have their calling fully figured out, but it helps when the person you're considering understands what they believe their long-term contribution should be to the world. Asking about a person's calling helps you to see what they value in life. You will see what makes them come alive and what drives them.

People interpret calling differently and may not know exactly how to answer the "calling" question. Here are some other ways of asking the "calling" question:

- What things are you passionate about in life?
- Money not being a factor, what type of work would you do for the rest of your life?
- What are you skilled at doing?
- What kind of legacy do you want to leave?

Those passionate about their calling seek to pour their hearts and souls into that calling over a lifetime. That's a major investment to say the least. Passionate callings come at a great cost! The more individuals exercise their calling, the higher the physical, emotional, financial, and chronological payouts. If the calling costs this individual physical energy, dedicated thought, money, and time, it will undoubtedly cost you as well if you two decide to unite in holy matrimony.

I ran into a friend of mine at a festival on a particularly hot day. He was perspiring and seemed to be a little winded. I asked what he was up to and he showed me the vendor booth where his wife was selling her custom made jewelry. He is not a jewelry maker in the least bit and has a completely different calling and career path than his wife. However, he bought into his wife's passion and worked the jewelry business as if it were his own. That's what happens when two worlds collide in marriage. You began to share in the calling of the other person, even if that's not your particular calling or passion. When a person describes his or her calling to you, you should then ask yourself if their calling compliments or conflicts with yours.

It's beautiful when a couple can share in similar callings and interests. Both feel a call to ministry or a call to politics and civic engagement. A husband and wife are into music performance and travel the world as musicians. A couple goes into a joint business venture and work side by side, building their empire. The whole family travels as circus performers (it's true for somebody!). This list could go on an on. The more a couple has in common, the greater the bond and potentially happier the marriage.

Like my two friends, they have radically different vocations and yet they find themselves invested in each other. When callings seem to be separate with radically different vocational paths, could you see yourselves happily supporting each other in those callings if married? Could you embrace her calling as your own, finding ways to invest in it? Could you push him further to pursue his dreams? Would you be comfortable with the payouts that come along with a person's calling: the time, money, energy, and mental space? If you feel that you cannot support a person's calling or it just doesn't compliment what you feel you are called to pour your life into, that may be a sign that this person may not be the best fit long term.

If a person is highly committed to a calling that would be in conflict with yours, don't ignore the hesitation you may feel. Your spouse should be your number one fan and supporter no matter what. What a lonely place it would be to have a spouse who doesn't support your calling and fan the flame of your passion! Find out what drives the other and see if you're willing to join in that ride.

CHAPTER 13
COMMITMENT TO GOD

This is by far the most important "C" in our *C Section*. Pursuing anything romantically with a person who neither (1) shares the same faith as you do nor (2) possesses a similar commitment to God is to start the relationship on the wrong foot. You already have enough hurdles to clear and obstacles to cross when fusing your life with someone else's life. Your faith shouldn't be one of those obstacles. Aligning yourself with a person of the same faith will at least give you a foundation on which to stand and will help you navigate other areas of relationship.

My first question on commitment to God is very simple and non-intrusive: *What church do you go to?* This single question opens the door for conversations concerning faith and spirituality. If a person says he or she doesn't go to church, I believe that's an instant red flag if you're a Christian. If a person tells you he or she goes to church but doesn't know the pastor's name, then it's safe to presume they are neither an avid church goer nor deeply committed to any particular ministry. Living out their faith through worship and community is not likely a top priority for them. If a commitment to God through gathering for worship is not a priority, you will see that there are other activities and causes that this person deems more important in his or her life. Those commitments will compete with your commitment to God and church.

It is common practice for avid church goers to give financially to a church through tithes (the first 10% of one's income) and offerings (free-will monetary donations). If you are serious about your faith and your spouse does not share the same faith commitment, he or she may very well give you a hard time when it comes to giving away money to the church. Money, as we have already discussed, is a major factor in marriage. Investing money into the church or causes that are precious to you but not as important, if at all, to your spouse will cause a myriad of problems.

Those deeply committed to a church give not only their money but also their time. I've seen first hand and have heard stories of couples who had issues because one invested much time in the church and the other was not as interested. Sunday services, midweek Bible studies, conferences, small groups, outings—several hours any given week can be dedicated to ministry. If both parties don't at least have a similar commitment or understanding, this too will also cause hiccups. One could even be blamed for giving more time to church than to the marriage and family. This type of lopsided time investment should not be the norm.

Chances are, if you're dating, you are corresponding with someone you have some level of acquaintance with (unless of course it's a blind date or online service). You may already know where this person stands in his or her faith with God; that is, you know that they are saved.[13] A good question to ask is, *How did you come to accept Jesus as your Savior?* Asking about their journey to faith in Christ will lead them to answer if they have in fact become a practicing Christian and it will testify of the impact that decision has made on their lives. This forms the foundation for everything else concerning faith.

I counseled a couple who was engaged to be married. One was a nominal Muslim and the other a nominal Christian. They were not

---

[13] Saved: rescued from sin and given eternal life by acknowledging and accepting Jesus Christ' death, burial and resurrection as payment for your sin.

actively practicing, but I let them know that if either of them decided to take their faith more seriously, they'll grow apart and find it difficult to navigate issues that are sure to arise, such as where to worship, what religious principles to teach the children, and dealing with conflicting teachings of the Bible and the Qur'an. I felt it to be unwise to officiate that wedding.

The Bible provides an entire chapter on marriage in Genesis 24. In this chapter, Abraham sets clear criteria for his son's future wife. Isaac was to marry a woman from Abraham's homeland and family, not from the place they were living as foreigners. Getting a woman with that criteria would ensure that Isaac marry a woman who believed like he believed, thought like he thought, served the God he served. To contemporize what took place, we could say the father wanted his son to marry a good Christian woman. Marrying a Canaanite would more than likely mean marrying someone of a different faith with different values and morals that aren't reflective of faith in the one true God. That would pose great problems for Isaac, who would be a pioneer of the faith not only for Jews but for Christians as well. Abraham had to connect his son with someone who would compliment him and not work against him.

In my particular faith tradition, having equal footing in Christian relationship is referred to as being "equally yoked." The concept is taken from 2 Corinthians 6:14, "Do not be unequally yoked together with unbelievers. For what fellowship has righteousness with unrighteousness? And what communion has light with darkness?"

Unequally yoked reflects an agricultural practice in which two animals (a team) were connected by a wooden harness called a yoke. A load was connected to the yoke so the team of animals could pull the load or plow the ground. When the team was unequally yoked, there would be one animal shorter than the other, or weaker than the other. *Got Questions* demonstrates what would happen in a case of animals being unequally yoked:

The weaker or shorter ox would walk more slowly than the taller, stronger one, causing the load to go around in circles. When oxen are unequally yoked, they cannot perform the task set before them. Instead of working together, they are at odds with one another.[14]

The context of this Scripture is not applying to marriage specifically, but this example is an appropriate application. Just as light and darkness cannot mix, or mismatched animals cannot effectively accomplish a task, it will be a strain for believers and unbelievers to fuse their lives together for a successful and satisfying relationship. There would be constant conflict because of the opposing principles and practices of the secular culture and the Christian faith. Marriage is the most important partnership there is, and great care to be matched and equally yoked should be taken. As Amos 3:3 states, "Can two walk together, except they be agreed?"

So, both you and your suitor love Jesus and serve His people. You give your time, talents, and treasures to God and His church. Both of you are involved beyond the norm. That's a great base! However, even with all of these commonalities, there is yet more to mine beneath the surface concerning the compatibility of two people's commitment to God.

While establishing common ground concerning faith is a great starting point, the faith experience of Christianity, or any religion, is not monolithic. Within Christianity, there are a variety of doctrines, beliefs, cultural practices, and varying levels of spiritual maturity. You may be surprised to see how divided people of the same faith can be. Asking the right questions will uncover those hidden beliefs and philosophies that are not as obvious.

---

[14]GotQuestions.org. "What Does It Mean to Be Unequally Yoked?" *GotQuestions.org,* 14 Feb. 2011, https://www.gotquestions.org/unequally-yoked.html.

How does one figure out what to ask concerning one's faith? One approach to deciding what to ask is to simply ask yourself, *What matters to me?* If it matters to you, it matters, no matter how trivial it may seem to others. If it matters to you, then you should ask it. Leave nothing to chance and don't assume that you both see eye to eye on issues. Most of the questions provided below hinge on the religious, but may overlap with certain questions asked in the *Convictions* section of the book.

- How do you feel about attending additional church services outside of Sunday?
- Do you attend any church conventions or conferences?
- Where do you stand on giving financially to the church through tithes and offering?
- How do you feel about Pentecostal charismatic types of church services? Are these words foreign to you?
- What kind of church do you go to?
- When did you receive the Baptism in the Holy Spirit? How do you interpret what that means?
- How do you feel about sharing your faith with other people?
- What type of Christian/Gospel music do you like?
- What other kinds of music do you like?
- Do you attend the movies?
- Baptism - Do you believe in sprinkling, pouring or immersion? In Jesus' name or Father, Son, and Holy Ghost?
- Tongues - is that gift for today or has it ceased?
- Dress up to church or dress down to church?
- Worship on Saturday or Sunday?
- Do both men and women preach, teach, lead at your church? Do you agree?
- How do you feel about Christians drinking?
- What's your opinion on Christians attending secular concerts?

These are just some of the questions that could be asked. No one will totally see everything from your perspective, but it is vital to agree on the fundamental doctrines and beliefs that help shape your faith and philosophy of life. The answers to those deeper questions may greatly help you in deciding whether or not to move forward.

I recommend thinking through the things that are close to your heart and writing them down. The two of you may not share the same level of attachment to the same issues. You may have some differences of opinion that are not deal breakers, but other contrary beliefs may pose an issue in the long term. That's why it's best to see where you two stand on any given issue of doctrinal belief. Aside from asking questions, I have found that general conversation, even about non-religious topics, will give you glimpses into someone's belief system and even deeper-held doctrinal beliefs. People may not always be able to articulate what they believe and subscribe to, but they will definitely demonstrate it through their actions and conversations. Be alert and active in your listening to catch the subtleties that reflect a person's heart and beliefs.

PART III: WHEN SHALL WE EAT CAKE?

Chapter 14
After you've learned to bake one

A lady was asked "What's your favorite thing to cook?" She responded, "Cereal."

I'm sure many of us can relate to that! I love to eat, but my cooking is nothing to write home about. Someone once told me, "If you know how to read a cookbook, you know how to cook." Pick up the cookbook of a bonafide chef and you'll find tried and true recipes for scrumptious creations with zero cooking experience (Are you getting hungry yet?). Cookbooks give you the benefit of other people's experience. They've worked hard to figure out recipes by testing out dishes and seeing what worked and what didn't. Following the recipe saves you time and potential meal disasters while making you look like a pro in the process. If this is true for making a dish or baking a cake, how much more for something serious like marriage?

There are many great *chefs* out there who've learned the art of *baking* a great marriage. These are the individuals who have gone through the school of marital hard knocks. They've gone through arduous times and joyful times. They've navigated the obstacle course of blending two lives into one. Years of marriage experience have taught them how to deal with inlaws, sickness, child rearing, financial conversations, disagreements, and first-year hiccups. Anyone navigating singleness, relationships, and thinking about entering into marriage would do well to talk with those who have gone through the trenches. This is not just good advice, but biblical wisdom. Proverbs 11:14 says,

"Where there is no counsel, the people fall; but in the multitude of counselors there is safety."

Sitting at the feet of competent counselors invites you to a well of wisdom and insight that would otherwise take you years of trial and error to learn on your own. Take time to ask your mentors the hard questions. Chances are very likely that they have asked your same questions and have dealt with the struggles you are currently encountering or will encounter. Such was the case with the apostle Paul and the Corinthian church, who had lots of questions for him regarding sex and relationships.

The book of First Corinthians is the apostle Paul's response letter to a church that had questions on a variety of topics, including singleness, marriage, and sex. We know this from 1 Corinthians 7:1-2.

> Now concerning the things of which you wrote to me: It is good for a man not to touch a woman. **2** Nevertheless, because of sexual immorality, let each man have his own wife, and let each woman have her own husband.

Paul provides us with some straightforward counsel in response to their questions:

1. Don't have sex with someone that's not your spouse (7:1)

This command addressed the issue of sexual immorality. The question was apparently asked about sex, and Paul set the parameters and context for sex: marriage. Some have compared marriage to a fireplace. Marriage is designed to house the flame of sexual passion, just as a fireplace is designed to contain a fire. But once you move the fire outside of the fireplace and into the living room, you risk burning down the house. Similarly, sex outside of the *fireplace* of marriage is a spiritual disaster waiting to happen. It is a sin against God because our body and spirit belongs to Him. It is also a sin against our own bodies and a sin against the person with whom we engage the action. Although the pleasure is only for a moment, the consequences can be far reaching.

2. Fulfill your spouse's sexual needs (7:3)

If you're not fulfilling your spouse's sexual needs, they will be tempted to search for other people or things to fulfill it. This will cause frustration and erode intimacy, as unnatural and unlawful roads to sexual fulfillment actually leave us empty.

3. Once married, you are not your own anymore, but you exist for your spouse (7:4).

As Pastor Tim Dilena put it, "When you get married, singleness dies."[15] Marriage is a calling to selfless service to one another. My grandfather would often say that your spouse's happiness is your number one priority. "When two people are working feverishly to make one another happy, you've got it made!" This was coming from a man with 60 years of marriage under his belt. It's worked for him, and I'm sure it will work for us as well!

We can summarize these three concepts Paul taught with three S's: Stop. Satisfy. Serve. Stop and think before yielding to the temptation of sex outside of marriage. Satisfy your spouse's need. Serve your spouse as if you belong to them, because you do. This is not to oversimplify what it takes to make a successful marriage, but packed into these three elements are the spiritual qualities that allow for people to thrive in relationship with each other. Choosing to stop, satisfy, and serve exhibits true love that will cause a marriage to thrive. Take a look at the qualities of love given to us in 1 Corinthians 13, the *Love Chapter*.

- Love is patient (waits no matter how long),
- Love is kind (generously serves others),

---

[15] Dilena, Tim. *Singleness Is a Big Issue*. Sermon published January 29, 2018. <https://youtu.be/TN3n1Q6zcyc>

- Love does not envy (happy for the successes and advancements of another),
- Love does not boast (not elevating itself at the expense of others),
- Love is not puffed up (humble and meek),
- Love is not rude (unseemly actions towards another),
- Love doesn't seek its own (concerned with the welfare of others above itself),
- Love is not provoked (not giving rise to anger or strong negative emotions),
- Love thinks no evil (does not keep a record of wrongs)
- Love rejoices not in iniquity (does not celebrate wrongdoing)
- Love rejoices in truth (takes pleasure in what is true)
- Love bears all things (covers the faults of others)
- Love believes all things (places confidence in others)
- Love hopes all things (expects the best)
- Love endures all things (longsuffering, puts up with everything)

Paul, the Corinthian church's counselor and teacher (and might I add, a single man) gave them some foundational recipes for success in singleness and in marriage. These insights, along with the sound wisdom of those who have navigated the often turbulent marital waters, will help ensure your success. Can you think of people in your life that can be sources of wisdom for you? Perhaps it's the couple that's been married for 20, 30, 40, or even 50+ years. It may even be someone in your life who has experienced the pain of a failed marriage. Consider a spiritual leader, pastor, or trusted Christian you respect to be a well of wisdom for you. Also, do your personal study with books, videos, and audio teachings on the subject. The insights abound to help you *bake a great cake.*

Jesus Christ was not beyond wise counsel. He sat at the feet of teachers in the temple to listen to them and ask questions. As a result,

Jesus began to grow in wisdom (Luke 2:46-52). Others who *sat at the feet* of teachers for instruction were Mary, the sister of Martha and Lazarus (Luke 10:39), and Paul the apostle (Acts 22:3). The concept of sitting at the feet means positioning yourself as a student to grow and learn from others. You will learn and grow by asking great questions to those who are experienced and have journeyed where you are trying to go. So whose *feet* will you sit at prior to marriage? Schedule some time with them over a meal or via a phone call. When things are official, investing in premarital counseling will serve you immensely. Don't take a chance. Get wisdom, and in all your getting, get understanding.

Chapter 15
When you don't mind breaking some eggs

Just about every basic cake recipe calls for the use of eggs. What is the purpose of eggs? Eggs serve as incubators, housing certain animals during their embryonic stages all the way through their completed development into a baby that's ready to be hatched. Eggs serve as an external womb, so to speak. Some eggs go full term to become baby chicks, while others' growth process is stalled, and they end up being used as food in one form or another. But in order to use the egg for food, you already know what you have to do: break the egg.

I believe relationships are a lot like eggs. Through spending time with a person, you develop things that almost feel tangible like friendship, rapport, memories, and a common bond. It's an egg, in a way. It's the atmosphere for something great to mature and hatch, but it doesn't always go to full maturity. These "eggs" are the product of a connection with a person which possess the potential for something great. Eggs are a metaphor for those things that are hoped for but not yet seen. The goal of such connections through dating relationships is marriage (or at least it should be). However, sometimes, those eggs never hatch.

Sadly, some eggs we have produced through well-meaning relationships can sometimes result in time wasted, complicated space, hurt feelings, and broken hearts when they don't develop into the beautiful swan that we may have hoped for. When this happens, we are just left with eggs that are good for nothing else but to be broken and used for another purpose. Breaking the egg doesn't always feel good. Here are just a few scenarios:

(1) After a few months or years of investing in a person, you arrive at that dreaded I-just-don't-think-this-will-work conversation.

   The egg breaks.

(2) You're a guy who has felt in his heart a certain person was the one you wanted to go after. You contemplate, you wait, then you pursue only for that person's heart to be enthralled with someone else.

   The egg breaks.

(3) There is an *old flame*. You all are lingering, having conversations here and there, with a small glimmer of hope and possibility. Then you find out he has moved on and is dating someone else with no real warning.

   The egg breaks.

(4) Your relationship went all the way to engagement, but stopped short of the altar.

   The egg breaks. And it hurts.

Breaking the egg can mean a shattered dream. Grief over the loss of a relationship or a potential one is painful as you cope with the emptiness that's left behind. Breaking the egg can mean *egg* on your face, embarrassment because of the failed relationship and looking foolish to those on the outside. The breaking can be embarrassing, especially if you were so confident about where things were headed. The breaking can be a blow to your ego, especially if someone is breaking it off with you. No one wants to look like the one being dumped or let go. Feelings of rejection and diminished self-worth can easily creep in.

Yes, the breaking is tough, but it can serve as a breakthrough, which creates a gateway for God to deliver to you what or who you need. Breaking is never easy, so it's important to know how to navigate through the breaking. Breaking may hurt, but refusing to break those eggs that'll never hatch can be just as frustrating because staying in the shell is of no real benefit to anyone. An egg shell can break because it's hatched, manifesting the life inside of it. It can break because what's inside of it is needed to become an ingredient for something else. Or the egg can break because it is mishandled and wasted. Eggs break. It is part of life.

No one wants to remain in the shell. People want to know if a friendship is going to become something special or nothing at all. No one wants the ambiguity of an egg with no direction. And we most certainly don't want to waste the opportunity to gain something fruitful from the broken pieces. When the desired results of a relationship don't manifest, something has to break and here's how we can deal with it.

Grieve it

I once heard author and professor Dr. Terry Wardle state that every loss deserves the appropriate amount of grief, whether you lost your favorite friend or your favorite pen. Grief is that unseen processor that helps us move through brokenness to wholeness. It helps us to say that what happened mattered, and the loss of it hurts.

Grief is not the absence of faith. Grieving does not mean a person has lost faith in God, as some would like to believe. Grief is the crucible that brings the pain to the surface so it may be skimmed off, just like silver when heated up causes dross (impurities) to rise to the top. Grief unearths the pain and enables us to deal with it so it can be removed instead of just festering in our hearts. In grieving, we can name the negative feelings and work through them. If you feel hurt, betrayed, disappointed, or even lonely, grieving helps you to acknowledge that.

In times of grief, I have prayed, "Lord, give me tears." Tears help to release the built up pressure allowing us to pour through our eyes the emotions that can't be articulated with our words. The psalmist instructs us to pour out our hearts before the Lord and trust Him in all times (Psalm 62:8).

It also helps in these grieving moments to talk to a friend. Most times, people aren't looking for answers, quick fixes, or unwarranted advice. They know what needs to be done and are aware of what's happening. They just need to talk it out and pour those feelings out to friends who will be willing to listen and not superimpose their will and ideas concerning the situation. I'm not speaking of having bashing sessions with a friend about a former interest! I'm talking about having real and honest conversations in which you share how you feel about the loss and prayerfully move forward in healing.

Trust God with it

I know that sounds so simple and maybe even a bit *Captain Obvious*. But truthfully, the fear of the future and hopelessness we may feel from breaking the egg will dissipate when we remember that (1) God is always good, (2) God has my best interest in mind, and (3) God works things together for my good. God is too good for us to remain in a state of despair about what was so bad. God's got you! You are in His hand. You are clay on His potter's wheel and He is making you into something beautiful. Give it to Him, journal it, pray it out, but whatever you do, make sure you tell God about it. He specializes in making beauty from ashes.[16]

Be transformed by it

All experiences are opportunities to learn and be transformed, no matter how good or bad they are. Experience is the university everyone is enrolled in. We have an opportunity to learn the necessary lessons or risk going through similar situations so that we can learn and change. Those tests in life we don't pass have a way of creeping back into our lives, forcing us to face them again and repeat them. So learn from your broken experiences. Reflect on them so you may learn and grow.

Are there any eggs you need to break? What things are you holding on to that aren't maturing and developing? What is keeping you from breaking the egg? I know it's not the easiest thing, but God's grace is present to help you. God will cover you and cover them. You may feel like the *bad guy* and experience the real pain of loss and embarrassment, but in the end, you'll release yourself and others to become who God needs them to be for their next season.

Not all eggs hatch into birds, but some eggs become ingredients in another dish. Are you willing to *break the egg?* That is, are you willing to sacrifice what you thought could be so that you can prepare for what should be? No one wants to miss out on what God has for them because they refused to break the egg. God will give you the strength and wisdom to do it. Your cake is depending on it.

---

[16] Isaiah 61:3

CHAPTER 16
WHEN WE'RE HUNGRY

It has been an ongoing critique in church circles (particularly African American ones) that people in church may not struggle with alcohol or cigarettes or some other noticeable vice, but they do struggle with the fork and the knife. Sometimes, the greater struggle is not "Will I turn up this weekend?" but rather "Will I eat two slices, three slices or the entire pizza?"

I'm being facetious, but I think we can *all* identify with eating because of other factors outside of actually being hungry. When it comes to answering the question *When shall we eat cake?* I believe there are some people who are cutting a slice but really aren't hungry. They're marrying, but a sincere desire is absent. They feel pressured or entitled for one reason or another.

In her book *I Deserve A Donut,* Barb Raveling presents several scenarios in which a person may eat even when he or she is not hungry. Here are just a few:

- Boredom Eating, when a person eats because they have a block of time with nothing exciting to do
- Emotional Eating, when a person tries to satisfy an emotional longing with food;
- Hopeless Eating, eating because you failed to stick to your boundaries so you give up trying
- Indulgence Eating, in Raveling's words "is an attitude that says *I want you, and I'm going to have you. I don't care if you're bad for me, I*

don't care if you're outside my boundaries, I just want you. And that's enough"[17] and

- Social Eating, when a person eats because everyone else around them is eating or they feel pressured by others to eat.

I read some of these and had to say *Ouch!* Why? Because I have experienced any number of these and I've felt the food struggle while trying to fast or be restricted in my eating. It is very striking to see how these scenarios fit into our subject on marriage. I think we all can agree that there's no use in being married if you don't really want to be. Yet, it happens all the time.

I've got nothing else to do

Some are *eating cake* because of boredom. They feel that marriage will bring the excitement that they are lacking in their lives. Now, don't misunderstand me. Marriage indeed is a wonderful thing. It is an amazing journey that God has ordained and people should be excited to marry. But marriage cannot fill the hole of a lackluster life. Marriage will have exciting moments, but nothing stays exciting all the time. No one's every waking moment is filled with excitement. There will be days that are mundane, bland, and downright difficult, but it does not make them any less meaningful. If you're bored with life now, you will likely be bored with life after marriage.

What brings about boredom? Boredom comes when we have time that is void of either meaningful pursuits or the proper attitude towards the pursuits that fill up our time. When we were children we would say "I'm bored. There's nothing to do." While you are in this time of singleness, what are you doing to make your time meaningful? Will you sit and twiddle your thumbs waiting for a spouse that may or

---

[17] Raveling, Barb. *I Deserve a Donut: And Other LIes That Make You Eat.* Truthway Press, 2003. 54

may not come or will you choose to start living now and fill up your life with something meaningful?

A man on a mission

Most people are familiar with the creation story of Adam and Eve. God created Adam and said "It is not good that the man should be alone; I will make him an help meet for him" Genesis 2:17. So God put Adam to sleep, took a rib from his body and created Woman, a suitable and equal partner to help Adam. As a father brings the bride and presents her to the groom, God presented the woman to Adam in the first marriage recorded in the Bible. That was an epic moment in the creation narrative, but it's important to see everything that happened to Adam while he was single.

> **Genesis 2:15, 19-20**
> **15** And the Lord God took the man, and put him into the garden of Eden to dress it and to keep it. **19** And out of the ground the Lord God formed every beast of the field, and every fowl of the air; and brought them unto Adam to see what he would call them: and whatsoever Adam called every living creature, that was the name thereof. **20** And Adam gave names to all cattle, and to the fowl of the air, and to every beast of the field; but for Adam there was not found an help meet for him.

Adam had meaningful pursuits during his season of singleness. He wasn't just sitting around bored and waiting on someone to come his way. He was engaged in some work that consumed his time and energy and was meaningful to the world around him. Adam was a zoologist and landscape architect. God gave Adam an entire garden to cultivate and tend to. God also had Adam name all the animals. Adam developed the first animal naming system and maintained a brilliant garden. He was tending to the things God called him to do while it was just him in the equation. These were no small tasks by any stretch of the imagination. Adam was doing big things while he was single. Likewise, our single years are great years to establish and do something big for God. While you are by yourself, you don't have to be consumed with what you'll be able to do when you're married. You can do some great things right now. If we wait for certain conditions "some day," we may never do something meaningful today.

Ecclesiastes 11:4 (NLT)
Farmers who wait for perfect weather never plant. If they watch every cloud, they never harvest.

Whatever we need in order to accomplish something big for God is either in us our around us. We have abilities, resources, people, and God's empowerment so we can accomplish things of great worth for God. When your eyes are focused on God-assignments, you will find a sense of fulfillment that will sustain you and keep you moving. When you are consumed with God-sized endeavors, it will keep your eyes away from the small stuff, killing the boredom bug.

While Adam was taking care of God's business, God was taking care of Adam's. He didn't have time to be consumed with boredom or the lack of anything to do. I'm not saying that moments of boredom won't come. They will. But when they do, they will be minimized because of the life-giving endeavors you are going after and the proper attitude and perspective you employ in those moments. Those moments of boredom will be less and less because you're filling the space with God and the glorious tasks that use your time, energy, gifts, and talents. Just like Adam, when we work on God's things, God will be working on our behalf behind the scenes.

I think that it's important to note that even when you get married, you will still need pursuits that bring meaning and purpose to your life. The addition of a spouse alone won't fill that need. Even in marriage, we must actively engage in our vocation, pursuing the meaningful work God has called us to. This will safeguard us against "boredom eating."

Everybody's doing it

The next scenario that motivates us to eat when we're not hungry is social eating. You feel forced to eat by others or yourself. Raveling pinpoints a few emotions that can accompany social eating. Firstly, people are expecting you to eat. As a result, you want to fulfill their expectations and please them. Secondly, you feel people will condemn you or get mad if you don't eat. You don't want to feel rejected, so you eat. I've personally experienced this numerous times. "Why aren't you eating?" and finally got a plate to quiet my critics. Thirdly, you feel you have a right to eat because everyone is eating. And lastly, you want to eat because you don't want to feel left out and you feel it's not fun unless you're eating, too. How does this look as it relates to *eating cake?* Allow me to share a personal experience.

A few years ago, many of my peers were getting married. It seemed like everywhere I looked someone was engaged and planning for a wedding. Within the span of a few short years I was either in or attending about seven weddings. No exaggeration. It was as if Cupid was working overtime shooting arrows. In moments like these, the pressure mounts to be married. Like the questions we looked at earlier in the book, people start asking, *You next? Got your eye on somebody? Sooo, when are we gonna eat cake? Everybody's doing it!*

Just like the social eating pressure, people are at times pressured by others to enter into a marriage covenant beyond their own will. Look at some reasons why people feel pressured to take the marital plunge. See if you've ever felt these emotions.

1. Everyone looks so happy and they're having so much fun. I want to join the fun.
2. If *they* could find someone, certainly I can. I deserve a spouse!

3. People keep asking me when's my turn. They're telling me it's time to get married.
4. People are making me feel bad for waiting so long. I've got to do something about this.

All of these statements are rooted in the social pressures to get married. People will always have their opinions about when you should get married, who you should marry, where you should marry, and on and on. Wise counsel is needed, but you don't want to govern your life purely by the opinions and whims of others. At the end of the day, you have to make your own decision and live with that decision. You have to wake up and look your spouse in the face every single day and decide to make it work. When things go wrong in marriage—and they will—that person who egged you on won't be there to help things along. Choose to live life and make decisions that will be in your best interest and be pleasing to yourself and God. Getting married just to please others can cause you to make a decision out of obligation and manipulation.

The Apostle Peter was speaking with a group of pastors and told them to lead God's people voluntarily and willingly with eagerness, not because you feel forced or constrained to do so (1 Peter 5:2). If you're in a relationship right now or even engaged to be married and you feel constrained and forced, do both of yourselves a favor a gracefully bring it to a close. I know that's easier said than done. I know there will be feelings of shame, embarrassment, and failure. You will feel that you let people down. But those things are rooted in what other people will think. "Till death do us part" is a long, long time to not get it right.

Are you really hungry?

People have varying appetites for wanting to be married. Not every hunger is motivated by God-honoring reasons. So what's the right type of hunger we need to *eat cake?*

1. We need a hunger to love someone like Jesus loves.
Ephesians 5:25 says "Husbands, love your wives, even as Christ also loved the church, and gave himself for it." This is referring to a sacrificial type of love that puts the needs of others above personal comfort and need. This type of love is unconditional and loves through the highs and lows, the good and bad, the peaceful moments, and the storms. This is agape love, the love that God Himself embodies. We are called as believers to love each other with this type of love.

> 1 John 4:7-8 (NKJV)
> **7** Beloved, let us love one another, for love is of God; and everyone who loves is born of God and knows God. **8** He who does not love does not know God, for God is love. **9** In this the love of God was manifested toward us, that God has sent His only begotten Son into the world, that we might live through Him. **10** In this is love, not that we loved God, but that He loved us and sent His Son *to be* the [sin-removing sacrifice] for our sins. **11** Beloved, if God so loved us, we also ought to love one another.

2. We need a hunger to serve someone like Jesus serves.
Jesus told his disciples about his selfless mission in Mark 10:45 when he said, "For the Son of Man came not to be served but to serve, and to give his life a ransom for many." We must be hungry to serve someone because it's in our hearts to help with no strings attached. Selfishness will destroy any friendship, especially a marriage. Successful friendships are give-give. Great joy awaits those who choose to serve others, living out their love in tangible and practical ways.

3. We need a hunger to partner with someone the way Jesus partners with us.

Jesus partners with us to carry out his mission in the earth by equipping us with gifts, abilities, and His Spirit. Likewise, we should be hungry to bring all we are to the table and use our unique gifts and callings to build each other and build something great for the kingdom of God. It's not about connecting with a spouse so they may help you build your personal kingdom and agenda, but it is about creating a supernatural team—a family—to carry out the great commission and impact the world for Jesus.

4. We need a hunger that finds beauty in a person, seeing them as Jesus does.

Let's not over spiritualize this thing. Beauty and attraction *are* a big deal. It's one of the first things that draws two people together. But it is the inner beauty that is long lasting and keeps people together. If we focus on the external only and are driven by passion to be with someone because of how they may satisfy our physical longings, we'll never be satisfied. Dr. Marvin McMickle writes, "Love and passion have a way of crowding out reason and reality."[18] An external focus will hamper our ability to think and reason soberly about our marital future.

When we have eyes to see what truly makes a person beautiful beyond aesthetics, we began to see our brothers and sisters as God sees them. They become more than physical objects for affection and adulation, but men and women who are valued because they are image bearers of God. In God's eyes they are beautiful, not because of their body type, hairstyles and clothing but because of the inward work of salvation. Humility is attractive, confidence is beautiful, and the fruit of the Spirit flourishing in a person's life is a lovely work of art to the eyes of the soul. When you can see people in that light, your hunger and desire is in the right place.

---

[18] McMickle, Marvin. 11

What's driving your hunger for marriage? People pleasing, authoritarianism, sexual drive, entitlement, selfish gain and FOMO (fear of missing out) are not proper sources of hunger to be married. Examine your heart for any *bad eating habits* so that you may avoid entering into relationships and covenants that are motivated by the wrong hunger.

CHAPTER 17
WHEN THE CAKE IS DONE

I grew up smelling the aroma of freshly baked dishes in the kitchen. Both my grandmother and mom were quite the cooks growing up. As a child, I always wanted to mimic what I saw my parents do. Trying my hand at baking was one of them.

My mom purchased a cookbook for us that had a recipe for each letter of the alphabet. I fondly remember the bakery item for the letter "A" – Applesauce Breakfast Cake. I was excited to try out my recipe book and make this dish that caught my eye.

We had all the ingredients we needed: milk, eggs, salt, sugar, butter, flour and, of course, the applesauce. The oven was preheated, the ingredients were mixed, and it was time to place it in the oven. We baked the cake and the aroma filled the house. In my haste, I took the dish out of the oven. After all, it looked golden brown on the outside and smelled pretty scrumptious. But one cut into the cake revealed that it was done on the outside but not fully cooked on the inside. It looked as if it were ready for consumption, but it needed some more time in the oven.

Sometimes, things can seem to be all set and ready to go on the outside, but there is still some inside work to be done before making the life-long commitment of marriage. What loose ends need to be tightened up? What issues need to be dealt with? What things need to be developed? What questions need to be asked? Only you can answer the question concerning the inside jobs you must take care of before adding another person to the equation. Those things that are not handled on the inside have a tendency to show up at the most inopportune times.

Many things could be happening on the inside that need to be addressed. There may be some character issues to work on. Maybe there are selfish tendencies, trust issues, impatience. Perhaps things like improving your integrity, keeping your word, increasing your work ethic, and a number of other character traits are ready for improvement. Do you possess some bad habits you know could drive another person crazy like punctuality, cleanliness, complaining, overspending, or over committing? Now, I'm not saying that you have to get yourself perfect before marriage. There are always areas of improvement, and you'll keep growing and changing even after "I do." However, we should be perfecting ourselves while we *wait for the cake*. We can maximize this time by taking advantage of the time we have to ourselves to improve in all areas. That may look like consistent time with God, working on our health by getting a gym membership or joining a fitness class, or improving our image and outer appearance with a closet purge and wardrobe change. Since we have to wait, we might as well make the most of it.

Take inventory

Spend some time with yourself to think and reflect on the things you could improve in your life. Think about improving in a few different areas:

- financial
- personal (physical health, image, space)
- schedule (how you spend your time working, serving, playing)
- spiritual
- educational (not just formal schooling, but also self-help, seminars, etc.)
- emotional

When you've listed areas for improvement, take just one or two of them and list about three action steps you can take to improve them. Note that some of these action steps may require additional action steps to complete the goal.

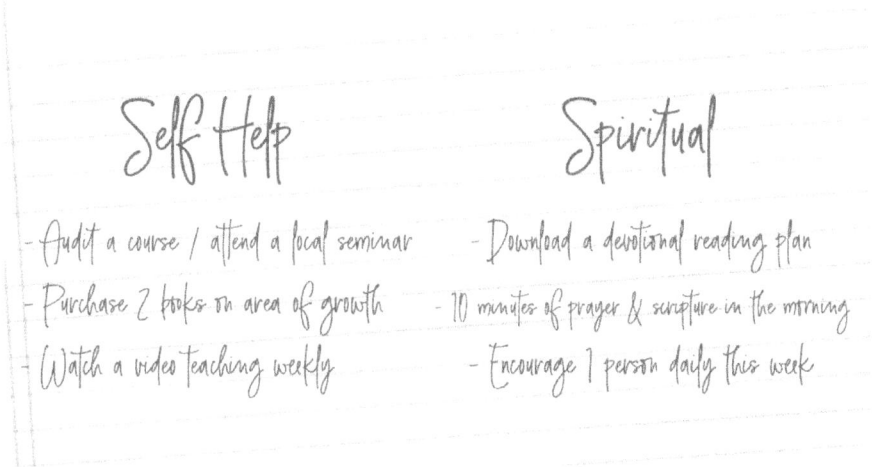

Self Help

- Audit a course / attend a local seminar
- Purchase 2 books on area of growth
- Watch a video teaching weekly

Spiritual

- Download a devotional reading plan
- 10 minutes of prayer & scripture in the morning
- Encourage 1 person daily this week

Put a due date on them once you write them down. What gets dated gets done!

There may also be some very specific and specialized areas of your life, such as your business, life goals, or another area you lead that needs improvement. Whatever it is, just jot it down. When you start improving in one area of your life, it will undoubtedly overlap with other areas and give you the motivation to keep moving forward.

So you've started working on yourself. Great! Things are going pretty well and at this point, you've accepted that you personally are not the holdup to being married. What a relief! But keep in mind, dealing with our own inward issues is part of the equation in waiting for the cake to finish baking. Another extremely important factor is simply waiting for the right conditions and the right person. Will we choose to wait until we find the person that fits our standards, "clicks" with us, and accepts us for who we are? Will we wait for the person with whom we feel at peace, or will we rush the process, loosen our non-negotiables, and try to work with what seems to be best at the moment?

Waiting for the cake to bake can seem like an eternity. Truthfully, the older we get and the longer we wait, it can become more tempting to lower our standards and expectations. The longer it takes with whatever we are pursuing, the more relaxed our standards usually become.

Think about your list of things you wanted in a spouse when you were a teenager. It was probably different by the time you reached your twenties. As a teenager, a young woman may have said, "I want him to be 6 '2, a millionaire, etc." But then she gets into her twenties and says, "Ok, he doesn't have to be a millionaire, but he needs a good paying job; he doesn't have to be 6 '2 but he has to be taller than me." By your early thirties, it's "Forget about the height. Just a nice and respectable guy with a cute face." Then come the forties: "Lord, just let him love God and like women." The older you get, the longer it takes, it becomes more tempting to relax your standards concerning a spouse.

Let's examine a 40 year-old single man in the Bible, Isaac. His story from singleness to marriage is found in Genesis 24. An entire chapter is dedicated to Isaac finding a wife.

> **1** Abraham was now a very old man, and the Lord had blessed him in every way. **2** One day Abraham said to his oldest servant, the man in charge of his household, "Take an oath by putting your hand under my thigh. **3** Swear by the Lord, the God of heaven and earth, that you will not allow my son to marry one of these local Canaanite women. **4** Go instead to my homeland, to my relatives, and find a wife there for my son Isaac."

> **5** The servant asked, "But what if I can't find a young woman who is willing to travel so far from home? Should I then take Isaac there to live among your relatives in the land you came from?"

6 "No!" Abraham responded. "Be careful never to take my son there. **7** For the Lord, the God of heaven, who took me from my father's house and my native land, solemnly promised to give this land to my descendants.[a] He will send his angel ahead of you, and he will see to it that you find a wife there for my son. **8** If she is unwilling to come back with you, then you are free from this oath of mine. But under no circumstances are you to take my son there."

9 So the servant took an oath by putting his hand under the thigh of his master, Abraham. He swore to follow Abraham's instructions.

(Genesis 24:1-9)

Now, let's unpack this here. Firstly, Abraham had the liberty to choose a wife for his son, so he sets the standards for the wife Isaac will marry. She had to come from a specific place and a specific family. As we saw in the previous chapters on questions to ask a person you're dating, it is important for you to share the same faith and be equally compatible spiritually.

The second standard Abraham sets is that the bride-to-be has to follow Isaac and live in Canaan with him. Language related to a woman following her husband is not very popular in an era of rugged individualism and questions surrounding gender roles in marital relationships.

I believe it is perfectly ok to have accomplished goals and possess your own things, choosing not to wait for a man or marriage before you start "living your best life." I encourage any woman to *do her thing*. Explore the world, pursue your career, buy a place to live, and do whatever it is you are passionate about doing. Do it big! But understand that when you get married, stuff changes. You submit yourself to the one God has ordained. That word submit is almost like a cuss word to some people. The reason why it gets a bad rap sometimes is because of the chauvinistic and domineering behavior exhibited by some men. Ephesians 5:22 says, "Wives, submit yourselves to your husbands." But this comes right after verse 21, which says "Submitting yourselves one to another in reverence of Christ." This a call for service to one another and mutual submission that honors Christ. Leadership in marriage doesn't mean "I'm lording over you." Rather, marriage should contain mutual submission that honors Christ and says, "we respect and love each other as equals." This doesn't negate a husband's leadership, it just shows that he has to be a servant before he can lead. Wives will be more apt to trust the leadership of the husband as he first loves her like Christ loves the church. She will follow the man who is going somewhere.

Abraham not only set a standard for the woman, but also a standard for Isaac. Abraham commanded his servant to not let Isaac go back where he came from. Why is this? Abraham was well acquainted with the promise of God. Abraham's last recorded words are of him rehearsing God's promise on his life. "God is going to give this land to me and my offspring." Abraham knew that in order for this promise to go forward, Isaac would have to live and raise his family in the land of Canaan. What we're seeing in this passage is that Abraham didn't change his standards because Abraham knew his purpose.

When you know your purpose in life and stick to your standards, you create a buffer against connecting with someone as a spouse who does not complement that purpose. If you don't acquaint yourself with your purpose and standards, it is possible that you could connect with someone who may work out as a spouse but will not fully complement who you are and where you're going. Personal standards help weed out the pool of people who aren't viable options. Abraham knew his promise and this gave him direction concerning Isaac's spouse.

Unrealistic Standards?

These guys were *getting up there.* Abraham was 140 years old. Isaac was 40 years old and had never been married. Abraham had what some would consider to be some unrealistic standards, especially at the twilight of his life. Despite their age, they waited patiently without compromise. I can imagine the conversation between Abraham and his servant.

> **Abraham**: "I need you to do a 450-mile camel ride to find Isaac a wife."
> **Servant**: "450 miles? That's pretty far! Why can't we go somewhere closer to find a spouse?"
> **Abraham**: "Nope! Go there and bring her back home."

Now, what are the chances that a woman who doesn't have a clue who Abraham's servant is will be willing to follow him back and marry a man she's never met? I think we can all agree that, on the surface, this was an unrealistic standard. However, it wasn't too unrealistic for God. God honored Abraham's standards and allowed each of those standards to be met. Now, if Abraham was 140 years old with these types of standards, and Isaac was 40, single, and waiting, we can still have standards–at whatever age we are–concerning the things we desire God to do in our lives. Abraham further shows us that we don't have to settle for less than we expect.

Like Father, Like Son

Isaac later had twin boys, one of whom was named Jacob. Just as his father had done for him, Isaac also set standards for whom Jacob should marry.

Genesis 28:1-2 (NKJV)
Then Isaac called Jacob and blessed him, and charged him, and said to him: "You shall not take a wife from the daughters of

Canaan. **2** Arise, go to Padan Aram, to the house of Bethuel your mother's father; and take yourself a wife from there of the daughters of Laban your mother's brother.

God also repeated to Jacob the same promise that was given to his father Isaac and grandfather Abraham. The promise, once again, served as a confirmation of the standards for which Jacob should pursue a wife.

Jacob arrived at the homeland and became acquainted with the servants of her mother's family and also the daughter of his uncle, a woman named Rachel. Jacob loved Rachel, who was a beautiful woman. Jacob knew this was the woman he wanted to marry and told her father that in place of payment for working for him, he would serve him seven years for his younger daughter, Rachel.

Genesis 29:20
So Jacob served seven years for Rachel, and they seemed *only* a few days to him because of the love he had for her.

Jacob found a woman that met the standards, and yet he still waited. You may find exactly what you're looking for and the timing may still not be right for moving forward. The cake is still in the oven. Jacob waited because of his love for Rachel. He kept his word and kept himself. Jacob's patience and discipline teaches us that true love waits. When we are driven by our unbridled passion and desires, they can override our discipline and sobriety. But when true love is in the equation, love that is sacrificial and giving, waiting becomes easier to do. Jacob could have chosen an easier and quicker route, but what's readily available and easy to attain isn't always the best thing for us. The sad reality is that many people have grown weary of waiting. They have given into the demands of a world that says, "Don't take your time.

Hurry up!" They ask the question, "What's the use in waiting any longer?"

In the process of waiting, it's important that we learn to manage expectations. We should always believe God for the best, believing that He will answer our prayers, even as it relates to a spouse. But we must also be alright with the possibility that God will not always answer in the manner or timeline we expect. We must not grow weary in these moments. If we do not train ourselves to manage expectations, we will grow faint in our hearts when things don't play out as we hope. Many of us are facing some sort of temptation, trial, or pain. You even feel like the clock is ticking. You're asking the question, *Why should I wait for the Lord any longer? I'm going to be a senior citizen before I get married."*

We wait, not only because we want God's best, but we also want to give our best. We wait because real love says I don't have to pressure anyone or be pressured into making a decision. Your waiting may be a few months, a few years, or several years. Your teens and your twenties may have passed, as have mine, and you are yet waiting. But resist the urge to rush the process and lower your standards. Take this time to grow yourself and allow God to do a work in you while you wait for God to work things out. God knows your desires, hopes, and dreams! Just wait on Him and He can do beyond your imagination. God's baking up something great for you.

CHAPTER 18
WHEN YOU'VE FOUND A FRIEND TO EAT IT WITH

I came across a photo on Pinterest of Winnie the Pooh and friends spending time together. The caption read, "We didn't realize we were making memories. We just knew we were having fun." That's a good summation of friendship. Those same feelings of warmth, ease, playfulness, and communion we find in our friendships should be the same elements we experience in a potential spouse. We should be able to enjoy each other's company as friends outside of the romantic and deeply emotional moments because they are just that–moments. No relationship or marriage is all passion, romance, and high energy. There will be lulls and calm times. There will be times when passion wanes and there is no romance in the air. There will be times when you need to capture that same friendship atmosphere that allowed you to spend time with your friends without regard to time, agenda, or any romantic expectation. True friendship will make a marriage last and be a sort of glue that keeps things together, even when the intense feelings of love begin to wane.

The way we look for spouses is to look for good friends. Good friends make good spouses because the foundation is built on that which goes beyond the physical and emotional. Friendship finds its criteria within character.

A friend makes you a better person

Growing up, I would hear my grandfather give this simple definition of a friend. A friend is someone who makes you a better person. Yup, that's it. When you're with that friend, you should become better and help make them better. If that friend is not making you better, then that's someone you'll do well to cut loose. But thank God when you can find a friend who is there to lift you, encourage you, and just simply make you better.

I'm reminded of a song recorded by Bebe Winans some years ago called *That's a Friend.* Those lyrics give a succinct, yet full picture of a true friend.

> A friend will always tell the truth. Even when it hurts sometimes.
>
> And a friend will always remain true. No matter what, when or why.
>
> And a friend will tell you when you're wrong. Still stand by your side.
>
> Best or worse, the friends go straight. They never say goodbye.
>
> Somebody who is faithful till the end. Someone the time has proved you can be there
>
> And if you call no matter where. Is everything okay? I am on my way
>
> Now that's a friend
>
> Somebody you can lean on, laugh and cry. Not only words but actions exemplify
>
> You don't have to have a reason why. I'll be there for you to catch you through
>
> Yes that's a friend[19]

---

[19] That's A Friend lyrics © EMI Music Publishing, Sony/ATV Music Publishing LLC

There are several qualities a friend can have and many things they can do to make you better and prove that they are a true friend. Here are just a few of those qualities.

Friends steer you towards righteous living

The apostle Paul spoke of people who knew God and His righteousness but refused to abide by God's righteous standards. Even worse, they approved unrighteous behavior in others.

Romans 1:32 (NLT)
They know God's justice requires that those who do these things (wicked behaviors) deserve to die, yet they do them anyway. Worse yet, they encourage others to do them, too.

Of course, that's no quality you want in a friend. We should desire friends who are going to spur us on to good works and pure living. As Hebrews 10:24 states, "And let us consider one another in order to stir up love and good works."

A good group of friends are going to encourage one another to do the right thing. If you constantly find yourself in a place of compromise with a friend, you have to really ask yourself "Is this connection worth my conviction?" Let me be the voice of reason and tell you that it's not worth it. It's enough work trying to fight off sin and abstain from anything that will weigh you down. You don't need any additional help to sin! I know it can be difficult to have a shakeup in your circle of friends. You may have a history together, grew up together, went to school together, or came through some trial or significant life event with this person. But keep in mind that extensive history doesn't give validation to the friendship if it is presently not adding value to your life.

A friend tells the truth when it hurts

Proverbs 27:6

Faithful are the wounds of a friend; but the kisses of an enemy
are deceitful.

Sometimes, the truth can hurt and feel like a wound on your
heart. It is a bruise to our ego because no one really enjoys being
critiqued and evaluated. The nature of the truth will cut us at times, but
it's not to harm us. The cutting truth is present to heal, much like a
scalpel in the hands of a surgeon. Friends will tell you what you need to
hear and not always what you want to hear. Good friends aren't "yes
men/women" or people pleasers. You want a friend to tell you when
you're making a bad decision, when you're going the wrong way, or
even when that outfit doesn't look quite right. This type of truth telling
flows from love.[20] You can trust it because you're aware that your friend
has your best interest and wants you at your best. Those are "faithful
wounds."

However, we must beware of the pleasant, yet deceptive actions
of others. The writer calls these deceptive actions "kisses of an enemy".
This verse gives us a foreshadowing to the betrayal of Jesus. A person
Jesus trusted and even called friend betrayed Him with a kiss. Judas
used a physical form of affection as a mechanism to turn Jesus over to
those who wanted to take his life (Matthew 26:49). Judas' actions were
deceitful, although gentle and loving on the surface. The kiss was not
true, but covered with betrayal, deception, and greed. To this day, I've
never met a person named Judas. His name has become synonymous
with unscrupulous character and betrayal, all because he was a bad
friend that abused trust.

There was a king in the Bible named Ahab, the king of Israel,
who desired to fight a war in order to reclaim his land (I Kings 22). He
invited his friend Jehoshaphat, the king of Judah, to fight alongside

---

[20] Proverbs 27:6. *King James Study Bible Notes*, Biblegateway.com

him. Jehoshaphat agreed but told the king to seek God's insight first. King Ahab did just that, or so it seemed. He asked four hundred prophets if he should go to war (prophets are people who are gifted to hear messages from God for people). All 400 of them affirmed his decision for war. But Jehoshaphat knew that something wasn't right. Although these prophets claimed to speak for God, they weren't really hearing from God. They only said what the king wanted to hear. Jehoshaphat asked,

> "*Is there* not still a prophet of the Lord here, that we may inquire of Him?" **8** So the king of Israel said to Jehoshaphat, "*There is* still one man, Micaiah the son of Imlah, by whom we may inquire of the Lord; but I hate him, **because he does not prophesy good concerning me**, but evil." (1 Kings 22:7-8)

King Ahab acknowledged that he knew exactly where to get a true word from, but he settled for the "kisses from an enemy" instead of the "wounds from a friend." Ignoring those faithful wounds, the piercing yet necessary words of caution, Ahab went to battle and lost his life. Be sure not to throw away friends who tell you the truth when it hurts, misinterpreting their discipline for abuse. The words may not feel good, but they are good for you.

Friends tell you the truth when it feels good

Your friendships will be terribly imbalanced if the only words a friend has for you are criticisms. I believe friends should offer much more praise than criticism for one another. If you or your friend can only offer criticism, you will develop a critical eye in which you look for things to be wrong. Excessive criticism is going to breed cynicism. You'll bend towards the negative, questioning people's motives and actions. Yes, we need constructive criticism from friends, but we should be more apt to give uplifting and encouraging words to our friends. We should not just tell the truth when it hurts, but tell the truth when it feels good.

Hebrews 3:13

But encourage one another every day, while it is called "Today."

To encourage a person is to strengthen them with the words you say. Friends will tell you truthful, life-giving words to build you up. Those words will shed light on your positive qualities and the great things you're going to be. A good friend will tell you when you're doing a good job. He/she will encourage you and push you to keep going and pursue your dreams. Friends see the larger role they are to play in your life; they know their role is to be bigger cheerleaders than they are critics. Friends embrace the attitude, "If you think something good, say it."[21] The truth shouldn't always hurt. The truth should feel good as well because it is encouraging us.

A friend is loyal

Proverbs 18:24 (NRSV)
Some friends play at friendship but a true friend sticks closer than one's nearest kin.

Loyalty speaks of dedication and faithfulness to a person or cause. Real friends show their faithfulness to the friendship, even when no one is looking. A loyal friend defends you in your absence, not allowing others to spew harmful and critical words about you when you're not around to hear it. Loyal friends are there when you need them. They seek to reconcile when issues may wedge themselves in and cause separation. Loyal friends see the friendship as greater than the temporary things that may be personally desirable but potentially harmful to the friendship. Do you have secrets to share, deep matters

---

[21] Pastor Craig Groeschel gave a sermon on encouragement during the Elevation Church Code Orange Revival, which inspired this thought. September 2016.

of your heart that you want to unload onto a friend? A loyal friend is built to handle those things and will not leak your personal business to other people. Proven loyalty builds trust and confidence, key ingredients that will be necessary in any relationship. Just as the scripture puts forth, a loyal friend will be closer than your nearest kin.

A friend makes great sacrifices for the friendship

> John 15:13
> Greater love hath no man than this, that a man lay down his life for his friends.

Of course, the ultimate friend anyone can have is Jesus, in that he laid down his life for his friends, you and me. Most of us will never be faced with such an extreme sacrifice of laying down our physical life for a friend. Although we may never cross that road, there are other ways, both small and significant, in which we can and should sacrifice for someone we call a friend. These sacrifices can take place through the giving of our time and resources.

Time

Today, I came across an email about how we use our time with those special people in our lives. "Time cannot be stolen, exchanged, refunded, stockpiled, or hacked. Time is extremely limited—and insanely in demand."[22]

No one is rich or poor as it relates to time. We all receive the same amount of time on a daily basis: 24 hours, 1,440 minutes, or 86,400 seconds. As a result, time is very precious and how you spend it (even more than how you spend your money, in my opinion) shows what you value and who you value. Sacrificing time speaks volumes for

---

[22] The 5 Love Languages Newsletter. June 19, 2018.

those you consider a friend. When you love and care about someone, you make time for them, even in the busiest of situations.

Motivational speaker and coach, Dr. Eric Thomas said in one of his videos, that whenever he sees his wife's name or one of his children on his phone, he picks up and answers, no matter what is going on or whom he is with. If he is busy, he'll still pick up and let them know that he will get back to them. He never sends them to voicemail. Now, that's called showing someone they matter through your time!

If a person is always too busy to talk, hang out, help, or celebrate with you, then he or she likely doesn't value the friendship as much as you do. There are some friends who will make time at the drop of a dime or make room in a busy schedule. I'm thankful for friends like that. A friend who is never able to make time for you may be safer in the associate zone.

Resources

A friend is generous with their resources, whether it be knowledge you need, sharing their connections, a tangible resource, money, or simply giving you that "heads up" for something you otherwise wouldn't know about. Friends aren't stingy but generous with their resources because they want to see you win in life.

One day, while Jesus was at a friend's house reclining at his table, a woman walked in and emptied an entire jar of perfume on him as a sign of honor.[23] The perfume was very expensive, totalling more than 300 denarii, which was equivalent to a year's wages. People ridiculed the action, but Jesus affirmed her, saying that she performed a good service for Him. This perfume she used to anoint Jesus represented her time, her energy, and her finances. She sacrificed her resources because of her deep care for Jesus. That's a friend!

---

[23] Mark 14:3, Matthew 26:6-13; Luke 7:36-50; John 12:1-8

Friends will make the big sacrifices and the small ones. Whether it's caring for you when you're ill, helping you through a rough season, or something smaller like helping you move or letting you borrow a cup of sugar for that homemade cake you're baking (do folks still borrow sugar?). Friends learn the art of sacrifice and inconvenience, realizing that those are seeds sown that will bring about great dividends, not only in their own lives but in the lives of their friends. When you've found a friend like this, you have likely found someone who may very well be worth spending the rest of your life with. Life is always more enjoyable with friends.

CONCLUSION

I'm on a plane ride headed home after spending some time in the Turks and Caicos Islands. There was a lovely resort there at which I was able to enjoy some leisure time. Water sports were available to the resort guests, so I decided to try my hand at kayaking. I strapped on my life jacket, received a brief tutorial, and then I was off to the races. After about 40 minutes into kayaking, I began having a difficult time turning myself around to head back to shore. In order to get back, I had to row against the wind. Little by little, I began to gain some ground and enjoy the ride. But not long after, I saw a man on a sailboat; the same man who gave me the tutorial and sent me on my way. He hollered out, with a smile and his island accent, "I come to save you!"

I chuckled because I didn't realize I needed saving. But he knew that I was likely having a difficult time coming back. He was right and I'm glad he came and towed me back to shore. He latched up the kayak and I joined him on the sailboat. It was an enjoyable, breezy ride back to shore on those crystal blue waters. What a sight to behold!

I share that story because all of us are navigating through some seasons in life. There are some areas we are challenged in and other areas we manage pretty well. When we have a good handle on things, it can be difficult to recognize that we may need some assistance. You may be merrily rowing your boat to shore and not realize that you are in need of "saving." Whether you're in dire straights as it relates to your singleness or cruising merrily along, I hope this book serves as a sailboat to get you to your destination smoother and more efficiently. Enjoy this season of singleness. Great things await you!

Works Cited

Adams, Rebecca. *Here's Why You Should Talk To Your Partner About Your Ex (Seriously).* HuffPost, 1 July 2014.
https://www.huffpost.com/entry/talking-about-your-ex_n_5533210

Dilena, Tim. *Singleness Is a Big Issue.* Sermon published January 29, 2018.
<https://youtu.be/TN3n1Q6zcyc>

GotQuestions.org. "What Does It Mean to Be Unequally Yoked?" *GotQuestions.org.* Feb 14, 2011.
<https://www.gotquestions.org/unequally-yoked.html>

Holy Bible, New Living Translation. Wheaton, IL: Tyndale House Publishers, Inc., 1996.

http://www.cogic.org/about-company/statement-of-faith/

https://www.census.gov/population/socdemo/hh-fam/tabMS-2.pdf

Keener, Craig S. and John H. Walton. *NRSV Cultural Backgrounds Study Bible*. Genesis 24:14. Grand Rapids, MI: Zondervan, 2019.

McMickle, Marvin. *Before We Say I Do: 7 Steps to a Healthy Marriage*. Valley Forge, PA: Judson Press, 2003.

Proverbs 27:6. *King James Study Bible Notes*, Grand Rapids, MI: Zondervan, 2019. <Biblegateway.com>

Raveling, Barb. *I Deserve a Donut: And Other Lies That Make You Eat*. Truthway Press, 2003.

The 5 Love Languages Newsletter. June 19, 2018.

The New King James Version Bible. Nashville, TN: Thomas Nelson Publishers, 1975.

Young. Ed. *Fifty Shades of They: Choose - Part 1*. Sermon published January 11, 2015. <https://youtu.be/VirGaFTDyiM>.

About the Author

Kellen Brooks is the pastor of Pentecostal Temple Church Of God In Christ, in Inkster, Michigan; which is the city and also the church he grew up in. He is an accomplished organist, pianist, and songwriter. He spends the bulk of his time playing and creating music, writing, public speaking, teaching, and enjoying the outdoors through his new found passion of running.

When Shall We Eat Cake?

THANKS FOR READING!

Visit KellenBrooks.com for new releases and upcoming dates.

www.ingramcontent.com/pod-product-compliance
Lightning Source LLC
Chambersburg PA
CBHW051732040426
42447CB00008B/1098